Shine

Ten steps to your child's b

TARA AISHA

Shine – Ten Steps to Your Child's Brightest Future

Author: Tara Aisha

Copyright © Tara Aisha (2022)

The right of Tara Aisha to be identified as author of this work has been asserted by the author in accordance with section 77 and 78 of the Copyright, Designs and Patents Act 1988.

First Published in 2022

ISBN 978-1-915492-58-6 (Paperback)

Published by:
Maple Publishers
1 Brunel Way,
Slough,
SL1 1FQ, UK
www.maplepublishers.com

CONTENTS

THANK YOU

Thank you so much for buying my book—well, it is now your book too. This feels so amazing, and I love that you are now reading the words I wrote for you. I am probably just like you: a parent, a working person who has their ups and downs in life, a friend to some, a child to my parents, and someone that gets it wrong sometimes, but also gets it right! I hope this book helps you and you feel better for reading it. I would love you to pass the message on, pass the book around, buy it for a friend, and hopefully, very soon, we all end up with a better life.

DEDICATION

I dedicate this book to my sons, my parents, my family and friends who love me daily and are always there for me. My father told me on many occasions, 'Go get 'em, kid, stop pussyfooting around and show the world who you are.' These are the words that spur me on. I also want to thank my four pets who sat with me and gave the comfort I needed to keep me writing these words, which I hope will change the world. Thank you to my editor for her kindness and patience.

Please note that some names have been changed to protect the identity of individuals.

IN LOVING MEMORY

I would like to pay a special tribute to my girl Nandi; she passed away not long after I finished writing this book. She was the best rabbit in the world, and she spent many hours on my lap as I typed. She was also the greatest therapy rabbit for my father. She will remain forever in my heart. She brought my family and I a great deal of happiness.

INTRODUCTION

I asked myself, *How I can write a book? How do I have the time?* Then I asked, *How can I not write a book?* I have made hundreds of mistakes and I want to make sure you don't make the same ones! I want to help you change your life. Through reading this book, I want you to have a better understanding of yourself and your happiness. In turn, it will give you a better understanding of your child and their happiness. The exercises, the knowledge that is in these pages will make life easier and happier.

I have always wanted to write a book, since I was about fourteen years old. Initially, I thought it would be a fiction book that I wrote, but somewhere inside of me, this book asked to be written. I look back at the words and think, where did they come from? I guess my longing, my desire, my need to get my message out was stronger than I realised. I literally started typing and then could not stop! The words appeared and rested on my page. I think being a teacher really made me want to help adults and children as I see so many parents asking me for answers.

I wanted to be a teacher since I was a child, and I have never wavered; it was a vocation for me. Going to university as a young single mum wasn't easy. It was, however, the best choice for my son and me. I wanted to prove that I was able to study and also give my son a better life. Yes, he was sometimes at lectures in his pyjamas with a cuddly toy, and he was often around campus with other young people who still remember us to this day. One of my closest friends from university remembers that my priority was always my son, and my hopes and dreams were for all children of the future. It is one of the best jobs in the world, albeit hard at times, and I have never regretted my training or being part of a world that shapes lives. Now I share these experiences with you.

I am not going to tell you that I wrote novels at twelve or that I read at the age of two! I am a person who has travelled through life making choices (good and bad), who cares deeply about others and about the world we live in. The many lessons I have learned have been from my eldest son. When he grew up, he kindly told me how much my unhappiness and the things that I got wrong had made him unhappy. This then influenced how I changed and grew as a mother, a teacher, a therapist, and how I ultimately found my own happiness.

I want you to read this book as though you and I are having coffee. It's like a conversation, and I hope you feel me supporting you as you make your way through the book. I have designed some worksheets that you will find at the back of the book, so that you can write down your thoughts. Do you know how powerful words are? Writing things down and looking at them really make us think. I have to say, even reading my own words made me remember my own journey more vividly and gave me quite an awakening.

What I want you to really take from this book is that you are not alone. You have this book; you have me rooting for you, cheering you on. I may not have met you, but once you read my book, we will be connected. This journey of yours does not have to be a lonely one, a scary one or a painful one. There is always an answer, always. I hope you find the answers in my book. Or, if not all of them, some of them. I hope your children see you with this book, that they know there are answers, and that they may use this book when they have youngsters of their own.

Love yourself completely and take this opportunity to get a cup of coffee and relax. Let the book take you to a place where you feel the contentment and peace that you deserve. Thank you for taking this time and I hope that one day I will meet you in real life.

My love goes with you, your children and all of those around you.

CHAPTER 1

HAPPINESS STARTS WITH YOU

Happiness is an inside job. I once read that in a shop window. It was on a card inside the store. I had no idea what it meant. I do now, dear reader. I want you to be happy, and I want the children in your life to reach their full potential. I want them to feel happy, content, and love life.

I am lucky enough to have two children. The first I had when I was very young, and the second one came along in my thirties. This gave me the advantage of the eldest one being able to inform me of all the things I had got wrong as a young mum. There were many things, believe me. But being a young mum was not the problem; I believe our chronological age is quite irrelevant. I was young, but I was also emotionally immature. Had I been young but in touch with my own happiness; things might be different. You will see from my book that age is irrelevant to me, but one's emotional and functional age and our awareness of others is paramount. I have met very immature sixty-year-olds and extremely wise sixteen-year-olds. I spent much of my twenties with the emotional age of a teenager. I was just unable to reach maturity. Many of us are stuck someplace, our minds are stuck at an age, and it is hard to move on. This was the case for me. This, in turn, hurt my children and made them unhappy. This was especially true for my eldest son as I was so unaware of the hurt I was carrying, which, sadly, passed on to him.

When he was small, I cried most days. Does this sound familiar to you? How many times does your child or the children you interact with see you laughing? Now think about how many times they see you grumpy, sad, tired, and frustrated. Is it a lot more than they see you smiling and happy? We are never going to get this time back, so we need to really think about how we want to spend each precious moment on this planet and with our children, whatever their age.

I am a mother, a therapist, and a teacher. The latter for over twenty years. I have seen children nearly every day of my life— my own, my relatives and other people's. I have seen adults and children through therapy. Did you know that 90 per cent of adults' unhappiness comes from something that happened in their childhood? Shall I tell you where most children's unhappiness comes from? Yes, you guessed, the adults in their lives. Shocking, isn't it? It is disturbing to me as a teacher, mother, and therapist. Shall I tell you where I learned this? Yes, I had read all the statistics, learned about them, but I didn't really get it. But I deeply understood it from one specific person: my eldest son. He made it very clear that my happiness influenced his. He is an academic genius, but his emotional health was impacted by me, and I cannot blame or look to anyone else but me. I am responsible. If I felt sad, so did he. Hard, isn't it? Once we accept that we have the biggest impact on our children, then things start to change—dramatically! If you are reading this book and your child is four or twenty-four, it makes no difference; you are still impacting them.

How many times have you said to your child, 'You are amazing, awesome, wonderful,' and they have looked at you and said, 'I am useless, fat, ugly'? Does this sound familiar? I look at the children I teach, each one of them amazing and inspiring. Even the badly behaved ones are pure and simply uniquely beautiful. Do they see it? Most of the time, no. People say that generations are changing. I agree that social media plays a part, but we are not changing that much. The conversations I heard twenty years ago in the classroom are the same as the ones I hear now. Children have low self-esteem and are upset over body image, grades, parental criticism and, most of all, relationships. I doubt that has changed since the youth of our grandparents, great- grandparents and beyond.

Guess where they learn this low self-esteem? Go and look in the mirror. Yes, it is you, shut the book if you want, but the truth is there. Do you know why? If you know, then great, if not. I will tell you. You give birth to or adopt your child. In their eyes you are royalty, you are heaven-sent. You are *everything.* Then suddenly, they hear and see you looking in the mirror, doubting yourself, with negative words. It literally is you just standing there being rude about yourself. Now they start to think, If my parent doesn't like themselves and I think they are perfect...what does that make me? They also start to question what you think of them. After all, if you gave birth to them, then they have the same shitty genes that you believe you have, or if you adopted your child, they think you chose them and you seem to think you are useless, so you must have crappy taste.

I was once called into my son's school. There I was told that he had very low self-esteem. I looked at him. To me, he looked like the most perfect child on earth; he was clever, beautiful, funny, and basically everything I ever wanted in a child. I looked at the teachers, looked at society. I blamed everyone but me. But sadly, I was where it started. I didn't know that at the time. It wasn't until my son was fourteen that he said to me, 'I used to hear you crying at night, telling yourself how useless you were.' The day I understood that my happiness affects my child's happiness is the day my life changed.

We moved house recently and I found all our home DVDs. I started to watch them and, of course, I was smitten when seeing my babies on the screen. But suddenly, I saw myself. I was completely amazed. It was like looking at someone else. In one of the DVDs, I was very young and at my eldest son's first birthday party. I was organised, in control, pretty, and confident. I realised that was how I looked to the outside world. But I knew that inside I was a ball of anxiety, insecurity, and self-hate. I wanted to go back in time and tell my-self, Listen, you are doing great, you go off to university with a child, you start a business, you are a good person. But that was not how I saw myself at that time. I also didn't speak to myself, in a good way. Of course, when I spoke words of hate to myself it was like a pin piercing my son's heart every time.

Let's go deeper into Step 1 of *Ten steps to your child's brightest future*. You make yourself happier. Read that again; it's important.

You make yourself happier. Say that out loud.

Don't panic; I am going to show you how. Wherever you are at this moment, I would like you to flip to the first work-sheet at the back of the book, labelled '5 things I like about myself'. I know, I know some of you will say, 'I like nothing about myself.' But listen, do you want to make your child happier, and do you want to make yourself happier? It is the same thing. The two go hand in hand, and I want to cut out all the steps I had to take to learn this and give them to you in this easy-to-follow book. You have got this and by the end, you are going to feel a much happier person and so will your children!

I don't mean temporary happiness like going off to Barba-dos, lying on the beach every day and eating your body weight in crab, although you might say, 'But that would make me happy.' It probably would, but you want a happiness that lasts long after you have left the golden beaches of the Carib-bean. I am referring to happiness that you can consistently feel, maybe not all day but most of the day. I have my down days, but I would say 80 per cent of my time is happy, and this, in turn, impacts my own children and those I teach and work with, in my therapy work.

At my son's last parent-teacher evening, the teachers said that his grades were at the top of his age group, but more importantly, they said what a happy, confident child he was. Bingo! I was walking on sunshine all day. That was when I knew that not only did I understand what makes our children happy but that I was successful in how I applied what I'd learned. That is why I am writing this book, to show you how to apply the steps.

So, write those five things down or, if you are snuggled up in bed, say them out loud. Your mind will try and stop you and make you think negatively but keep going. Do you know we have around 50,000 thoughts a day, and eighty per cent of those are negative? Research carried out by the National Science Foundation published those figures in 2017. Can you imagine that 80 per cent are not doing us any good? How sad is that? You can change this and, in turn, change the happiness of your child. You need to say those positive thoughts out loud. So, when you look in the mirror, be nice about yourself; your child is always listening. You think they are not...but they are.

My youngest is a school-aged teenager. I thought he was busy playing a video game when I was on the phone to my mother. I had a whole conversation thinking he was oblivious to what I was saying because he was in gaming land. I came off the phone and about two hours later he said, 'Why did you think Aunty Lucy didn't like you, last year?' What??? How on earth did he hear or remember that? It is because they are always listening, and they are always aware of you. You are their sun, their earth, and their moon. No matter what they say to you. That is the truth. They might seem to despise you sometimes, they might have tantrums, but you are the centre of their universe. You need to be stable and happy in yourself, or you are faced with a rocky ship and children who don't love themselves. So, *you*, dear reader, you need to love yourself. Oh yes, I am aware; I sound like a completely cheesy hippy. I am a hippy but not a cheesy one.

Let me break this down even further. Imagine right now that your six-year-old self walked into the room. Just picture it in your head. Look at that child and tell them that they are fat or ugly or useless or unlovable or stupid. It is hard, right? That is what I mean by self-love. You need to say things to yourself that you would want your six-year-old self to hear.

When I started school, I was the only brown child there. I remember a boy saying to me, 'Why are you brown?' I looked behind me and thought, Who on earth is he talking to? I wasn't brown. I was the same pinkish colour as my mother, I thought. I felt this boy was deluded. I had to confirm with my mum that I was brown. I am mixed race, so I am sure that is where the confusion happened. I was a cute little girl and slightly overweight. I was fine with all of me. I liked the way my tummy was squishy, and I liked the way my knees were rounded instead of bony. But others didn't like me...it seemed a boy in my class decided my new name was Little Fat Wog. Yes, that is what he called me most days. He told me I was ugly, looked like a pile of poo and should dye myself white. Guess what? I believed that boy. Suddenly the self-love stopped, and I wanted to be white. I wanted to be blonde, and I wanted to be thin. I believed that boy and I kept that with me for many years. I didn't tell my parents because I thought that they would be upset or ashamed. I thought they must be so upset that they had given birth to a little fat wog. That is the badge I wore, and I wore it for years. I felt worthless, and this was passed on to my children. So that boy's words impacted not only me but my children too. How sad and ridiculous is that?

I go back to my original point. What would you say to six-year-old you? What would I say to six-year-old me? I would not say she was a little fat brown wog. I would tell her that she is so much more than that boy's opinion. Whose words do you need to expel to start changing your thought pattern? You need to start changing those words today. If you hear yourself saying horrible things to yourself, picture yourself as a child in front of you.

I heard a friend say once, 'Oh, it's my 40th, I am just an oldie.' Label yourself and that is what you become. So, label yourself with good things. I never care about my chronological age and never tell people how old I am. I dress and act however I like. I still shop at Topshop, and I still dance around the room. People always think I am five or ten years younger than my age, but I don't want to be put in a box of 'Oh, now you are this age, you should be wearing a twin set.' I have friends of all ages, my youngest friend is twenty-eight, and my oldest friend is ninety. Our chronological ages are irrelevant, and my friendships are not based on age but on how much we get on. If you feel like dancing around Aldi, then do it. I say to my children all the time, 'Just be you.'

We are possibly only here once (I can't confirm this) but let's make the most of it. I wake up thinking I want to make the most of this day. I do have my down days; of course, I do but remember I am teaching my children how to cope, how to be resilient. I have made many mistakes, of course I have, but I need to forgive myself for those days. I remember my university lecturer saying to me, 'Tara, there are two things to remember as a teacher and as a parent. If at the end of the day every pupil is alive and healthy, then you have done a good job.' He continued, 'if they are those two things you can start to focus on and ask yourself if they are warm, loved, listened to, and fed, then you are smiling. If they are sleeping in a safe place, you have done a good job as a parent.' Basically, keep your child safe and keep them happy.

It is paramount that you keep yourself happy and safe. Part of Step 1 is to make yourself happier by being nicer to yourself. When I was a teenager and into my 20s, I was obsessed with my weight. I weighed myself five times a day. I was underweight and often exhausted. It was not a healthy attitude for my child. This led my eldest son to be brought up by a mother whose happiness was completely reliant on what the scales said. I am now a healthy weight, but the young me would say I was overweight. I train myself not to look in the mirror and default to saying, 'Tara, you are fat.' Instead, I look at myself and think you are a UK size 12, healthy and strong. I swim and I walk for miles. I have hips and a bust. I choose to like these things, but I still have days when that boy from kindergarten creeps in and tells me that I am unacceptable and below par. I tell him to bugger off. I look at Tara and love her, really love her, every part of her. Loving her means my boys love themselves. It means the children I teach love themselves and those I see in therapy. Who is your 'boy in kindergarten'? Right now, make the decision that they are not going to impact the thousands of lives you are intertwined with or, more importantly, the lives of your children.

I remember when I had given birth to my second son only six months prior to this day in question, I was three stone over my usual weight and quite tired. I remember I watched a programme about feeling good. I decided to wash my hair and put on make-up. I also decided that I was pretty awesome. I had two beautiful children, a good job, a business and I really did feel it, like a warm glow inside and out. I went to London for a course I was on, and I was chatted up by taxi drivers, men at the station and even the chap running the course said he had never met anyone like me! I was at my heaviest, had not slept properly for 6 months but my inside allure, my confidence was erupting from my pores. Compare this to the experience from years earlier in my 20s. I was a UK size 10 with glowing long hair but asked out only twice in 10 years. My self-esteem was rock bottom. This is the difference.

It is not about the outside; it is the inside. Happiness, beauty, that glow, really is an inside job. So, your mission is to start looking in the mirror and *finding* everything you like about yourself. Imagine you are looking at that 6-year-old you and compliment them. Put your favourite song on, dance around the room. Put on a funny film, forget the world, and laugh. Make yourself a coffee, tea, hot chocolate and just bathe in the fact that you are you. Your child will see this. You might not think they notice, but they will. Others will notice that glow and smile, even if you don't want to. Smile because eventually, you will want to without trying.

Shine

Your happiness and your own self-love are the greatest gifts you can give your child. Step 1 is over well done. You can keep writing things you like about yourself, add new ones. You can share these with me via my website, the address is at the back of this book.

CHAPTER 2

BE THE CAPTAIN

I was emailed a letter right before I started this chapter, and I want to share the significance of it with you. It was a letter from a teenager to her parents, written by Dr G.L. Schmelzer, PhD. Truthfully, I couldn't read it at first and had to start and stop as I kept crying. It made me think of all the children in my life. The letter reminded me of how hard teenage life can be. The hormonal shifts, the fight to stay in childhood some days and the need to be an adult on other days. It made me think of my own children—the younger one has now reached his teenage years— and of my own younger days.

Teenagers are not personally trying to hurt you. Please remember that. They have all this power and have no idea how to handle it. They are changing both physically and mentally. They need us to stay strong. Last night my younger son got upset over some school things he'd lost. He was really unsettled and took it out on me. I had to remember that this was not about me but his own fears, worries and needs. It is not easy if we are tired or worried about our own situations (work, family, etc.). I had to go out into the garden and take some deep breaths and remember that it is not personal. It is just him changing and growing.

My message still stands from Chapter 1; we have to be in our own power, our own confidence to help the children we love. When my eldest son was little, I used to think that teenagers didn't need looking after. The letter reminded me of how hard teenage life can be.

I thought they reached thirteen, and basically, your job was done. What a naive and silly girl I was. In fact, thirteen is when the hard work starts. They need you to be more confident and happier because they may be slowly slipping off the edge.

My sons have never said they hated me and, to be honest, I have not had any horrible teenage rows with my boys. I have had some times when I could not connect with them and that has been my fault. The younger son is now a school-aged teenager and I thought it would be easier the second time around, but it isn't. I still make mistakes and I still feel hurt. The trick is not to take things personally. Easier said than done. None of it is personal. That is the lifeboat you must hang on to. If they are angry with you, take it as a compliment, they feel safe with you. The exercise you are going to do today is to write your own parents or guardians a letter. Your parents may still be alive and around, or they may have passed away. My parents live nearby and are reading this right now. I put them through hell when I was a teenager (sorry, Mum and Dad, especially Mum).

After a bit of meditation and sitting on my own, I tried to 'remember' what it felt like when I was a teenager. I sat down and wrote a letter to my parents, but I got into my teenage mindset. So, I channelled my inner fifteen year old! She had a lot to say. I had forgotten how feisty she was!

Spend ten minutes doing this and you will feel differently about your own teenage children. Also, you will start to know what to do to make them happier. You don't feel old, do you? I still feel about fifteen. Children think anyone over the age of thirty-five is ready for the old age people's home. We need to remind them that we were teens too. I got up and danced to 'Smells Like Teen Spirit' last week, in the living room, and surprised my younger son! I also put it on at the end of the day at school and got my whole class jumping about to Nirvana. We laughed a lot and felt absolutely buoyant. All the form group are teens!

I kept a diary when I was a teenager. I looked back at it and it then informed the letter I wrote to my parents. I believe if you can challenge that inner teen, you can begin to understand that none of what children say or do as a young person is intended to hurt you. They are just in a very confusing place. I hope my letter helps you to start yours. You don't need an old diary to spark it off, though, just a bit of meditation and channel that teenage you!

This is what I wrote.

Dear Mum and Dad,

I don't know why you won't let me stay out late. You don't understand that other people are doing it. Why can't you let me? Why don't you get what it is like to be young? You are so old. I felt Mum's 40th birthday was miserable, and I wanted to go for pizza. Why can't you remember what it is like to be me? I want to be free. I want to marry Jo and set up a house and just be free. You will never understand this, as you have obviously never felt like I do.

Reading my letter—which comes from similar sentiments in my teenage diary, although obviously, my younger self did not write as eloquently as I do now—it did make me realise some things. I may have been a teenager, but I was still very much a child. I had no concept or understanding of why my parents wouldn't let me out. I didn't understand their fear and they just seemed completely hopeless. I was so young and unable to see it from their perspective. It wasn't my fault; I was a child in a growing and changing body. More than anything, it is important to listen to and communicate with our young people.

Children of all ages need boundaries. We all do. It makes us feel safe. If you don't have boundaries as a parent, then the child feels unsafe, and it won't be easy for them to listen to and engage with you. They need to feel that you are the captain and can lead them in a loving, supportive way. Teenagers need this more than anyone as they are in an ever-changing body, a foot in childhood and a foot in the adult world. We need to be the secure and loving parent no matter how choppy the sea gets and how much we are fighting to remain a good captain!

Both my children were toddlers who had a lot of tantrums. I was that mum who stood in the supermarket as my child screamed. My eldest once had a tantrum on the roadside when we were walking home, and another mum had to come and help me calm him down! I remember my youngest son once had a tantrum in a large department store during a two-minute silence being held. I looked at him and me in a mirror; he was red-faced and so was I. Then I realised, I am the captain of this rather rocky ship, time to set my boundaries. It was not easy. We had weeks of him pushing against them, but at the age of five, he was voted the best behaved and calmest child in the kindergarten class. It was not easy, and setting boundaries takes work, but it does pay off. I was never a parent who shouted, but I would sanction their rewards. My sons loved when I read to them. So this method worked beautifully for both of them as a reward. I am an English and drama teacher, so when I read bedtime stories, I put a lot of effort and accents into the whole affair. (I am going to be a fantastic grandmother one day, reading books to my grandchildren.) If one of the boys misbehaved, there would be the first warning. On the next warning, a page was removed from that night's storytime; they were horrified as they loved their stories. There has never been raised voices or any physical reprimands. This has made them calm and resilient. I am the same when I am teaching, I am not a teacher who shouts or makes my students feel unsafe.

I have taught thousands of children and the comments from Ofsted (an educational body in the UK that come into schools and make sure teachers are working hard) have been that I have outstanding relationships with pupils. I have worked in special educational needs (SEN) schools, urban schools, and independent schools and through it all, I have realised what teenagers need: boundaries, time, care, and your honest love for them. They also need to see you as an example.

I have been a teacher for over twenty years and observed one huge thing. When children are badly behaved or anxious or unhappy, so many parents blame the school, friends, relatives, social media ... but who is the first carer, the first teacher? It is you. I am sorry to tell you but look in the mirror and you will see the biggest influencer of your child. Forget the Youtubers who are actually paid to be influencers; you are doing it daily and all for free!

I once had a couple come to see me on parent-teacher meeting at my then school. They wouldn't sit together, and mum had brought her new boyfriend, so all three were there. The child was next to them. He was an only child, a lovely boy and very intelligent. And he was really frustrated. His mum and dad couldn't speak to me without arguing and the boyfriend threw in a few choice words too. What do you think the child thought of this? He was conditioned to think it was acceptable behaviour and he was able to emulate it. So, it was no surprise that he was swearing and had been in fights with peers. He was a highly intelligent child, but he later left school, unexpectedly. That child was destined for great things and whether he got there, I am not sure.

If you don't want your child to smoke, swear, eat badly, etc. don't do it yourself. Try to only have the best habits possible. I know that we are human and of course, we all do things that will not be deemed great. I used to swear a lot as a university student.

(I am not proud of this) During my student days, I would have other young friends around and sometimes we forgot little ears could hear us. One day my son and I were in a Woolworths store, and he must have been about three years old, the cutest little thing, and he went up to a shop assistant and said, 'Where the bloody hell are all the toys?' Of course, she laughed, but I was mortified. Choose your words and actions carefully; you are being watched!

I was a very emotional, sometimes anxious young mum. I was not always a good role model for my eldest son. As he got older, I realised I needed counselling for my own hang-ups. I became steadier in my own mind, more of a stable role model. If you feel that counselling could be helpful, then go for it and tell your child that you are doing this. (Obviously, make sure they are old enough to understand.) It shows them that it is ok to ask for help.

You are their example. Show them that you are reading this book, try leaving it on the living room table. They may never read it, but they know you are making changes.

None of us are perfect; I know that and have made hundreds of mistakes. But one thing I do know is we are the captains of the ship we run. If the cabin crew are running riot, then we need to sort it. This means setting boundaries and leading by example with maturity and consistency.

I also want you to think about self-care. Sleep, food, hydration. Yes, I know we read about it, but do you know lack of sleep can cause some catastrophic effects. Make sure you are sleeping; this keeps you calm. Take vitamins, eat healthily. I don't mean drastic diets but food which helps you mentally. I cook dhal once a week, it has lentils and peas in it. It costs £1 to make and feeds us for two days. I add rice, 49p, and salad, 94p. So, for two days we are eating for under £3. You can afford to eat healthily, and you can and must afford to look after yourself. You are the captain of the ship, and your health impacts the cabin crew! We will talk more on self-care in Chapter 6, so get the kettle on and keep reading.

The last thing I am going to tell you in this chapter is *laugh*. Yes, it seems so simple, but I often laugh at myself. I make a mistake and I think, Right, try again next time. Laughing releases so many good hormones and the thing we are worried about seems less painful or worrying. In fact, my dad said to me that he had never seen anyone who laughs so much and finds the energy to smile at most things! If things get worse, go into the garden and laugh. If everyone is still alive, then you can laugh and know that tomorrow is another day. The rest of it will be ok. I have suffered great trauma in my life, but now I think to myself, everyone I love is alive and well and I have a home, a roof over my head, and I can laugh at some of the most difficult things as they pass. *I am safe and I am more than enough.* You are more than enough too. Keep saying that, keep remembering it and your teen will too.

CHAPTER 3
MAKE TIME FOR YOUR CHILDREN

I do know that making your child happier by spending time with them (not buying them lots of things) is a big step towards real joy.

Ask each one of your children to write down five things they would like to do with you. Give them parameters like a budget and not further than say ten, twenty or however miles away. Also, tell them that it can't be anything dangerous. Say that you are going to do it this Saturday, or whenever you are able to. It must be this week. Do not cancel it! To get you started, I've created a timetable for you at the back of the book, marked Chapter 3. I hope this will help you to plan some lovely things with your children. You can photocopy it or just fill it in, and then you can let your children see that you are planning some quality time with them.

I remember one day my eldest son wrote that he would like to go swimming, have a muffin and go for a walk. The pool he chose was not my favourite, but it was his. If your child has this time with you, it makes them feel special and loved. Now, what happens if you have more than one child? I have worked as a teacher, and I have also worked in a pupil referral unit (PRU). There are normally five or more students in a PRU class, and I manage to give them ALL time. You can do this, and you will as you have made a commitment to yourself and your child/children.

What does this do for a child? It tells them that you care and that you are willing to spend time with them. If you have several children, put a time limit on it. If you are a single parent, then you may need to ask someone else to care for your other children. There is always a way. I have a friend who has four children, and she is a single working mum. She manages to give each child a bit of her time each weekend. If one of your children wants to paint your nails but you have a baby and a toddler too, do it after the younger ones are asleep. I know you might be exhausted. I know exhaustion. I went to university with a young child and was often doing essays at 2 a.m. in the morning. I also did cleaning and babysitting to pay my way.

If there is a will, there is a way. I know if someone said, 'Go for a five-mile run,' you might make excuses: washing needs doing, there's ironing, etc. If someone says, 'Go for a five-mile run and there will be £2000 handed to you at the end,' you will find a way to go. We can always find a way if the incentive is there. I remember another friend who told me she didn't have time to go for a daily walk. She made up so many excuses; it was unreal. Let me tell you her excuses: her eighteen-year-old son needed help with homework (all the time, really?). Her parents needed their shopping done (every day, really?), work was busy (she worked two days a week). So, you see what I mean; excuses are just that. Everything is possible.

When we don't want to do something, we make excuses. This is not healthy or good for us. Therefore, it is not healthy or good for our children. Make a decision and stick to it. You have made a commitment and you need to see it out until at least the end of this book, if not beyond. You are building happiness for the rest of your life. It is worth it. I promise you. It is not just your lifetime but that of your children and their children too. You are changing the world just by reading this book and following these lessons. You are changing the lives of your future generations and your legacies that are yet to come. These methods do work. I have run parenting courses at work, therapy sessions and followed this approach with my own children. It works if you follow the steps. You might feel deluded or upset, but at some point, this is going to filter into the foundations of your child's future life and yours!

Remember you don't have to be a superhero—the things you can do with your children can be really small, even just buying some popcorn and watching a film. It can be splashing in puddles, dancing in the rain, going for a walk, going swimming, cooking, painting, just go for it. Whatever their age—four, fourteen, twenty-four—there are very cheap or free things that you can do together. Just spend time with them and that is the best gift you can give them. Put a time limit on it if time is limited at the moment. But whatever time you do have, *put away your phone.* My children hate me talking to them while I am checking my phone. It is rude and unacceptable. Also, put your phone away when eating. How many times do you see a family out for dinner with their phones out? Remember, you are the captain of the ship; you take your phone out and then so does everyone else! In ten years time, your children will be teenagers or will have gone off to university or left home to have a family of their own. Your phone will always be there; your child will not.

I look back at my eldest son's childhood and I wasted it on worry. I was always worrying or texting people. I miss him now that he has left home and wish that I had savoured our time together more. We did do some lovely things together that were free or cheap. We loved swimming and cycling, and I think the times we did those things were vital to his good mental health. As I said before, I got it wrong, I still do sometimes with my younger son, but I have learned and am learning every day. I get it a lot less wrong than I once did! It is important to forgive yourself if you are struggling, forgiveness is very empowering and important for your child to see you grant it to yourself.

Teens love to talk when they want to; this isn't when you want to necessarily, or have time. Take the time for them, please. I promise it will help. That email can wait, the cleaning can wait, that text can wait, but sometimes they can't. My children don't like small talk but often connect with me on discussions to do with history, politics, and ethics. I was completely bemused when my children said those are the best conversations we have and the most fun. I think these discussions often get heated, but they love them. We are spending time together, connecting. Find the things your children like and connect with them.

CHAPTER 4

LOVE YOUR INNER CHILD

So, dear reader, you bought this book so you could make your child or children happier. But there is a child in your life who you have neglected for many years, I am sure of it.

It is your inner child. I know that we hear that phrase so often, inner child work. It reminds us of eighties feel-good movies. I used to think it was rubbish until I met an extraordinary lady. I won't give you her real name, but let's call her Diane. She changed my life in many ways. I was so used to ignoring my inner child and I began to live like a thief stealing that child's happiness.

Think about the grumpiest person you know. Just picture them in your head. Ok, got it? Do you like them? Do you have to see them often? Well, I guarantee you if we had a time machine, that person was not born grumpy. At some point, they were a bouncy baby. So were you, come to that. Therapists believe that around five or six years old, the average person is likely to consciously remember some sort of trauma; for some, it may be nothing big. It could be having to speak in front of a whole assembly. For others, it will be life-changing. It might be sibling rivalry, a cruel word, bullying, or far worse, abuse of some kind...but five or six is the age that things start to change emotionally. This age is when we start to form our personality traits that are not inherent, and this can be formed using what we know.

That five- or six-year-old still lives in you. Oh yes, I know, I know, you are fed up with this therapy claptrap. I am proof that the inner child resides very deeply in us, and they impact our life every day. This, in turn, impacts our children.

My children are living with the demons of my inner little girl; I am living with the demons of my parents' inner children, and so are you. So, let's make a change for our inner child and for our own children. Remember, being happy is an inside job. We need to look after our inner child and when we do, they will be happy and then those around us will feel this happiness. Nothing that happens now has anything to do with now—that sounds weird, doesn't it? It is all from the past. You are probably laughing but, believe me, it is true. I was like you and believed it could not be so. It wasn't until I saw Diane that I knew that I was dragging my poor little inner child into the present with all her hurt and sadness.

She kept believing that she was a little fat brown wog. No matter how thin I have got (and I have got very thin in the past, to the extent that my hair started to fall out), or how many compliments I got, I was that little brown fat wog. No matter how many qualifications I got, I was the girl who struggled with bullying at school, and no matter how many relationships I had, I never felt loved. I always believed someone better was round the corner.

I felt like everyone who was around me could do better. This was relationships, friendships and even my children. I believed there was a better mother out there for them.

My inner child was so used to being let down by the outside world that she pre-empted negative situations, people-pleased, and, most of all, she would make up lies about herself. One day I was in a shop with my eldest son and two women came over. They had not been kind to me. Left me off of invitations as I was a young mum, and generally gossiped about me because of my lack of money, poor clothes and my struggle. They came over, 'Oh wow, how are you?' I looked at them with fear. How was I? I was the same as I was most weeks. I was starving myself to be thin, financially poor, and generally feeling lost. I didn't want them to know that. In actual fact, I had much to be proud of. I was a young single mum doing something worthwhile, but that was not enough, in my eyes. I was training to be a teacher, my son was happily playing with his teddy, and actually, we were not doing too badly. I am not proud of what I did. I made up a story. I made up a life that I thought would impress them.

'Oh great, I must tell you, I have started dating a young head teacher, called Nick.'

Their eyes opened wide. 'Yes, he is lovely, and he is taking my son and me on holiday.' They did a lot of oohing and aahing and looked suitably surprised and even a little jealous. I mean, who wouldn't be? What a life I was portraying. I can feel the sadness now as I write this. How pathetically sad. Why didn't I see myself as I was? A beautiful young mother, with a beautiful son. A young woman going to university against all odds and doing very well. A good person who cared about others, was never a gossip or unkind. I could not see that then. I saw myself through their eyes, through the boy in kindergarten's eyes, through Mrs Donnelly's eyes (the maths teacher who called me stupid in Year 3), through the eyes of my son's father who told me, I was useless and unlovable. So, I gave myself a new persona. A headteacher would only choose someone great, right? Right. I mean, it must signify that I am great.

In fact, I made up someone that I wanted for my inner child. I made up a life that I wanted for her. The life you dream is the life you must give your inner child. You must find out what they are saying. Why are they upset? Why are they so angry? They might be angry or upset because you are not listening to them. My inner child has wanted to write this book for years. I didn't listen to her. I was happy to ignore her. Ignoring her meant I suffered headaches, bad periods, weight issues, and pure hatred for myself. Writing this book and seeing Diane weekly and then training as a therapist myself has meant that my inner child knows that I listen to her. I am at a healthy weight, sleeping better, and am more at peace. I have boundaries, I have good friends, and most of all, I have happy children. They see that I have unpicked my life. Whatever is happening now that is really painful, it is *not* just to do with now. Ask yourself this? Is it a relationship, your boss, your friends? Keep asking yourself, who is bringing up these triggers and what is your inner child asking for? I have been through all of this. I have had very painful relationships, horrid bosses, traumas, and worrying times, but all of it is has been worsened by how I feel about myself and my past trauma.

If you love yourself, then everyone else can see this, you are great to be around and then they have permission to be themselves too, to love themselves and to be who they want to be. If you love you, then your children will love themselves. So I want you to go and get some photos of that little child. Put them up and tell that child that you love them every single day. If that little child was next to you now, what would you say to them?

I know what I would say to my six-year-old inner child. I would say I love your brown skin, your cuddly little self, your beautiful kind heart, but most of all, I love how you love the world. My six-year-old inner child loved life and people. She loved life. She was so happy most of the time, and she was beautiful. We can let the world judge us, but no one will judge us more than we judge ourselves.

Stop judging yourself today. Do it for everyone. If you do, then that little person or young person who is your child will do it too. Start a pattern that rolls into your grandchildren's childhood. Start it today. So what if you look in the mirror and see grey hairs, look at those eyes, look at the smile. Focus only on the good. Ten years ago, I thought thirty-five was old. Now I look at thirty-five- year-olds and think how young they are. Ten years from now, you will look at photos and say, *WOW, that gorgeous person is me.*

I give you permission from this day onwards, let's make a pact, to love yourself, to feel beautiful, to love your inner child in every way possible. Spend time with them, meditate on them, indulge them, tell them you love them. A man told me last week that he prefers blondes and milky white skin. He started the sentence with, 'No offence to anyone but I prefer...' That is all good. That is his opinion, and his opinion is not mine. It is ok for someone to feel that way, but it doesn't have to mean that is your truth, nor should it affect your opinion of yourself.

If that boy in kindergarten was saying to me again, 'You little fat brown wog,' I would say, 'Actually, my name is Tara, Miss Aisha to you.' He must have hated himself to call me that; I was just a projection of his own hatred. Stop projecting your own hatred of yourself onto your children. Start projecting love. You are a loving parent to them and to that little inner child. Go make your inner child happy, right now, and you will see how much life will change for you and the children in your life!

CHAPTER 5

LEAVE THE PAST BEHIND

This chapter is about rucksacks. Not actual rucksacks but metaphorical ones and the past that we carry with us. If you are carrying the past around, then so is your child. No matter what you say or do to hide it, they see it. Having recently got Covid; I had to stay inside for ten days, as did my younger son, who also contracted it. We were both ill, but it meant I was in the house for ten days with just my thoughts. I felt vulnerable, tearful, and alone. I did everything I should do as a mother; I took care of my child, and I made sure he felt better each day. What I failed to do was look after my own mental health. I was tired and unwell myself, so I should have made myself aware of it. Rested, drank more water, and ate better, because as the days crept up on me, my mind went to its default position, focusing on the past.

I had traumas in my teenage life that left me feeling empty. I will touch upon one of those traumas later in the book. These traumatic situations caused me physical and mental pain. I had to seek a therapist to help me with these things. Safe to say, these traumas haunted me. Why did these traumas haunt me, I hear you ask? The answer was I was tired, and I was low. I looked around and there was the rucksack... in the corner, asking to be opened. What happens if we don't look at the past and challenge it to leave us? It remains and it comes back as a million emotions. If we ignore each emotion, it comes back and says, 'Hello, I am still here.' That trauma then becomes your child's trauma. This showed itself to me during my period at home, being unwell and isolated from the world.

As a therapist, through my training, I can literally see people's trauma as they walk through the door. I see it in their body language, their eyes and their smile. A child, your child, is very perceptive. They can sense if you are in a bad mood, if you are tired, sad…they are so tuned in to you and even if they cannot verbalise it, they will do it in another way. I had a very difficult pregnancy with my younger child and a difficult labour. I was left on a chair to give birth, I said I was in labour, but the staff in charge said I wasn't. Two hours later, I asked the nurse for help, and she told me to sit down. I said the baby was coming and seven minutes later, he was out. I suffered complications that I later learned could have killed me. That left a really bad feeling inside of me, and I felt extremely vulnerable. I had panic attacks and was afraid to leave the house, afraid to leave the baby. I would carry him everywhere. I still have remnants of that trauma now. He, in turn, didn't sleep and had screaming tantrums for three years afterwards. He was sensing my fear. Children sense our fear much more than we know. I have seen it in my own children, in those I teach, and most of all, as a therapist and coach.

Rachel came to see me about her child Roxanne, who was often tearful and regularly missed school. Both mum and daughter wanted to see me together and also have sessions apart. When I saw them together, there was a shared anxiety between the two of them. They would look at each other and wait for the other to answer a question. I asked Roxanne what was going on; she said she was being bullied and she didn't want to go to school. I asked Rachel what she felt was going on and she would give her thoughts; this went back and forth with neither of them meeting in the middle. Rachel said that she thought Roxanne was just being oversensitive. It was a difficult dynamic; body language changed throughout the conversation. I asked Roxanne if she would be happy to have hypnotherapy as well as neuro-linguistic programming (NLP), which I offer. She said yes, she would like that.

Roxanne attended my clinic and, when she was in a re-laxed state said, 'Mum's partner Luke used to hit her. I was scared. I don't want to go to school in case Luke comes back and hurts mum.' I was amazed when I asked Roxanne, after our session, about Luke and I found out the answer. Ra-chel's partner Luke had not been in their lives since Roxanne was two years old. Roxanne was now fourteen! Roxanne had no conscious memory of Luke, her mum's ex-boyfriend, and could not believe she carried it around with her. This was a complete shock to Rachel also. Roxanne was anxious about something that happened twelve years ago. She was carrying it in her subconscious. Rachel was carrying it around too. She would make reference to 'that time' or 'it's better just the two of us'. What are you carrying around? Who or what is in your rucksack? Clear it out, see a therapist, meditate, journal, come on one of our courses at Wellness Stars(my therapy clinic and wellbeing website), but whatever you do, clear it out. It will slowly eat away at you and your child if you don't face it and bin it.

One of the worst cases of carrying around the past was when I met Thomas. He had tried to take his own life. His mum brought him to me when he was seventeen. She was beside herself and couldn't sort it out. On the surface, Thom-as had lovely parents; mum was a nurse and dad a lawyer. They had a good marriage and lived in a lovely house, and all seemed well. Thomas said he felt like he was not good enough and wanted to just leave the world. It made me very sad, and I asked Thomas's parents if we could work together as a family. They were slightly hesitant and asked why they needed to be part of it all. I said it would help Thomas. Both parents were dubious of hypnotherapy. They had seen TV shows and thought that being hypnotised meant being out of control. I explained that it is merely a way of going into a relaxed state. They would always be aware and if there was anything they didn't want to say, then they would just tell me. It was not being 'out of it', as Thomas' dad said, merely being in a trance and relaxed state.

I left it with them and didn't hear anything for five weeks. Thomas had run away for twenty-four hours, but thankfully he was back and they knew they needed to do something. Thomas liked me and said he wanted to work with me. I was able to do hypnotherapy on all three of them and nothing astonishing came to light. We did another session, still nothing, until the third session. Thomas's mum was always late for our sessions, and she found it the hardest to relax. As I started, I could see her body language changing; this session was going to be different. It was in a way that was not immediately obvious, but I did have a gut feeling about it from her body language. Sadly, she had been sexually abused by a neighbour and it had left her frightened and broken. She had no conscious memory of it. All she knew was that she felt scared, depressed at times, but did not know why. She would often overeat and then starve herself. She was never completely relaxed...never 'at home' as she called it. Her periods were heavy and sometimes, she hated being a woman. She had hated her pregnancy as she was so sick, and after Thomas, she refused to have any more children.

This was a huge breakthrough and Lydia, Thomas' mum, looked ten years younger as she finished her session. She cried and sobbed. It was not the end of her releasing, but it was the start. Once she started to release, so did everyone else. It was like she was the tight coil, the unspoken pain which lived in the family. John opened up to me about how Lydia hated affection and he often felt rejected. Of course, Lydia had not known why she felt this way. Thomas began to heal. He had three sessions of hypnotherapy with me, and twelve counselling sessions with a young people's coaching programme, and we also did some NLP together. If we carry a wound, it shows up elsewhere and hurts those around us, especially our children. It is not easy unravelling pain, healing a wound, but we all have them. There is not one single person on earth who doesn't have wounds. We all have our wounds, and they live inside us and they come up in different ways.

Clara came to see me with Lizzie, her daughter. Lizzie was getting into trouble, running away, meeting unsuitable partners, failing school. It was difficult for the whole family and Lizzie's four siblings. I asked to work with both Clara and Lizzie. Clara was not keen. She had Lizzie and her siblings when she was young and felt that Lizzie was not listening to her as she hadn't listened to her mum in the 1990s. Clara was Spanish and from a very strict Catholic background. I asked Clara if we could try to see if she felt she was holding anything in that might hurt Lizzie. She was really angry at this, 'Lizzie is doing this. It is not my fault.' I reassured Clara that none of this was anyone's fault and no one was to blame. We are all just finding our way. She seemed to calm down and agreed to a session. Clara was remarkably receptive to hypnotherapy and on her first session, she opened up. Her father had left the family home and her mother had no time for her. She felt unloved, ignored, and dismissed. Her self-worth was so low that I almost cried myself. I could see six-year-old Clara begging for love and attention. It was a very emotional session and I have to admit I had to cry when she left the room. She had let go of so much. She had another two sessions, and this impacted her daughter Lizzie in such a positive way. It impacted her in a way none of us could have imagined: she got straight As at school, she joined a chess club, she helped her siblings with things. She was peaceful, grounded, and, dare I say it, extremely happy!

The final session with them both was so different from our past meetings. They came in holding hands! Clara told me how proud she was of Lizzie, and they had been doing more things together. They got their nails done and both had got highlights! Their body language and their facial expressions were so different. Clara had started swimming and showed off her toned arms. Both seemed to be thriving in self-care. There was a bounce in their steps. Clara told me that a bus driver asked if Lizzie was her sister and she said, 'I am like a young girl.' Clara let go and released, and this sent a ripple throughout the family.

What are you holding on to? What have you not released? Whatever you are holding on to, so is your child. If you are suffering, then so is your child or the children in your life. So, look at yourself today; by locking things in, you are causing yourself pain both emotionally and physically. I was lucky to see Tracy Stone around five years ago. She used hypnotherapy to help me clear out my own rucksacks. If you would like a good hypnotherapist to help you clear your past anxieties, she is your person. Her website is: www.limitlesspotential. co.uk

When I was seventeen, I met my friend Neville. He was a beautiful soul and really wasn't meant for this world. He was older than me by a few years, and loved art. He could draw so beautifully and was very creative. He had the most terrible home life. We didn't hear this from him, we heard about it from other people and we tried to ask him about it, but he would never admit to it. He was beaten weekly, told he was useless, and that the world would be better without him. We didn't know these things, only his brother knew. At the age of twenty-three, he died. He left this world, and I was one of the last people to see him alive. I now, as therapist and teacher, see that he was in the most dreadful pain. He lived a life of terror and abuse. Who do we blame? His parents who left Neville? His grandparents, who then mistreated him, despite being his legal guardians? How many generations do we go back? Neville's parents and grandparents could not have been happy people. This is not the way the world works. If you are feeling happy, content and relaxed, do you go and make other people's lives a misery? It is only the people who are suffering who try to make others suffer. So, the ripple goes on. What ripple do you want to pass to your children, grandchildren and great- grandchildren? Think about it right now. When I feel a moment of sadness, I think about what Neville would say. I still see his smile, and I know he would want me to be happy and follow my dreams. His death changed my life and made me even more determined to make mine count and to change the world.

As I mentioned earlier, I suffered traumatic experiences which shaped my view on how much I wanted to help young people. One of those experiences happened when I was sixteen, I went to a disco with my friends. I was attacked and beaten up so badly that my own parents did not recognise me at the hospital. I lay in that hospital bed and wanted to know what sort of people could do that. Ironically, fifteen years later, I taught the daughter of one of the people who hurt me. Talk about the past coming to haunt you. I found out many things about the family and, as you can imagine, I understand now why that particular person beat me with such force. She had put my head through a glass window and told me she wanted me dead. Her family life had been terrible and so was her child's life (the girl I ended up teaching). The generations were just repeating themselves. We, as a society, need to help each other. We need to reach out and help one another. Hurt people hurt others. Make a decision today to change the past and move forward in the future with love and kindness and teach our children that way of living.

Trauma in us can lead to scars that are very clear to our children. If you are angry or upset, this seeps through into your everyday life. Children watch how you interact with people. If you swear at the driver in front of you, if you argue with the shop keeper, if you are rude to the waiter taking your order, your child watches and learns. They watch everything and then they repeat. I was very angry for a very long time about being beaten so badly that I could have died. My anger was apparent even when I walked along the street. I felt scared of people; I could be unfriendly and unkind in my mannerisms. Of course, I was not a bad person; I had just had something bad done to me. The only way I could cope with it was by being angry and keeping the world away. So lead by example. If you want your child to be happy, then you must be happy. If you want to show your child how to do this, then lead by action. If finding happiness is by going outside and running around and getting exercise, then get up and go for a walk with them. If you want your child to stop worrying, then you must start looking after your mental health. If you want your child to be polite and considerate to others, then you must be too. Carrying around your anger and trauma is not going to help anyone, especially your child.

A good example of this is understanding our triggers. I was often bullied by a boy at school who would put spiders in my bag, down my jumper and even in my lunchbox. I had a great fear of spiders for a very long time. When I became a young mum, I was even more terrified of spiders as I lived alone with the baby and there was no one else in the house to get rid of them. I don't just mean a little bit scared; I would scream if I saw one. When my baby was very small, I remember one day there was a spider on the stairs, I wouldn't go down until it had gone; we both camped in my room! That is how bad it was. I then realised I had to be brave and face my fears; otherwise, he would inherit this same fear. I called it spider training and I do it with the children at school too. It wasn't easy; please don't think I am a martyr, and I had a few screams, but I succeeded. I can now hold a spider in my hands and not scream. In fact, I quite enjoy it and I truly had a huge phobia. If you want to release a phobia, try hypnotherapy. It is amazing and you will be so relieved and free!

Today I want you to be honest with yourself. How big are your fears? What is in your rucksack? This may be something you can't do alone, and if you can't, then be honest with yourself and get help. I know this is not easy and it takes courage. I know you have determination because you are reading this book and want to make your child happier. If you can and want to, then I would like you to do some journaling. Get yourself a lovely book and write it all down. Just start writing. What am I holding inside, and what is in my rucksack? Remember, you are your child's hero, do it for them as well as for yourself.

When Jean walked into my therapy room, she was smiling and cheerful. I was really feeling the good vibes. She was one of those people who lit up a room. I felt her sunshine everywhere. I asked what she felt I could help her with. She was silent...I could feel the room and hear her heart almost beating like a drum. It wasn't until she looked up that I saw tears in her eyes. She told me that she had come to see me as she had lost a baby. I was really sorry about that. She explained that she had never told anyone about this baby. She had been pregnant at a young age, and no one knew. She had lost it and had to take herself to the hospital. I was horrified and wanted to throw my arms around her. She was still grieving for this baby despite having three daughters and was now thirty-nine. She said her daughters felt her sadness every now and again. It happened particularly whenever anyone had a baby. She said she did not want to impact her children, so she came to me for help. I knew she was a brave person, and I knew I could help. She had never recognised the pain she experienced, and all alone. We had to go back to this and start healing. Jean is a lot happier now and often stays in touch. I have to say she is a good example of someone who wants to get rid of their rucksack.

When you journal, let yourself go, write freely. Write it to yourself or to a friend. I was surprised when I freely write, without stopping, how much comes out. It is all in there. If you can't do it yourself, get help and let your children know that if they are old enough, don't hide it from them. Go to a therapist, hypnotherapist, yoga teacher, whatever helps, do it! My children know that it is perfectly healthy to use a therapist and there is no stigma around it. I used hypnotherapy and relaxation techniques to get my son through the worst symptoms of Covid. I have helped him with sleep issues and will also help him when he takes his GCSE exams in the future (these are UK exams that children take at sixteen). My eldest is a little reluctant to let his mum help him now he is grown up, but I will keep trying!

I want to end this chapter by reminding you that you are more than enough. You are a warrior, powerful and strong. You can do this. You must believe in your own strength to rid yourself of that rucksack. You will have been carrying it around and surely you need a break? You, your children, your inner child, those around you need to see you letting go. I promise you will look younger, healthier, and more in control than ever before. People will comment and it will empower them. You will start a ripple effect; you will change lives. Most importantly, you will change the life of your child and of you. I saw a meme which said, 'I love you. I know I don't know you but if people can hate for no reason, then I can love for no reason.' This post had so many likes and it amazed me how much we all need to know that we are loved. I ask you to love yourself, love others and keep that ripple going. Until the next chapter, I love you, pass it around!

CHAPTER 6

SELF-CARE

What does self-care mean? Ok, let me put it like this. Do you make sure your children are well-fed and clean? That is you caring for them. Now let me ask you, who cares for you? Well, it is you, and if you are not caring for yourself, then it shows a lack of love. Things like washing your hair, bathing, all of these are self-care. As a parent, how often do you put yourself last? If the answer is often, then I am afraid to tell you that is just no good as it is teaching the children around you to do the same, that putting yourself last is acceptable. Before you had children, you probably spent money on yourself, spent ages getting ready to go out, met with your friends, and generally, life was all about you. Then you become a parent and you put your children's needs before your own. I understand that. I am a parent myself, but what I cannot do is put my needs last. My self-care is vital to their good mental health.

How does self-care show how we feel about ourselves? It shows that we hold ourselves in high regard, not bottom of the list, but right up there with our children. They are at the top of the list and our own self-care should be right up there too. It shows we have love for ourselves.

I had the misfortune to become friends with someone who had serious mental issues; they were later diagnosed with having narcissistic tendencies. While being friends with this person, I lost the real me; I lost all love and respect for myself. I look back at photos of myself from ten years ago and it was frightening. I had cut my hair myself (nothing wrong with doing that, but I had done it in a way that said I don't care about myself), I was very much over my optimum body weight, which is not healthy for someone with asthma, and I looked very pale. I am mixed race, so for me to look pale must have meant that I was not going outside, therefore my children were not going outside. I look back at that time as a very painful period in my life, but I am also grateful to that person who manipulated me so much and hurt me. Without that pain or challenge, I would not be who I am today. I grew in a way I have never known, and I realise that many triggers from my younger years were still there. I made erratic decisions which hurt my children, and I barely recognise the person I was back then. I had lost myself as I had done with my very first boyfriend. I had lost my personality and was not someone I recognised anymore. It was like watching a TV show and not recognising the main character, who was me.

I need to be a healthy, happy captain of my ship. I need to keep my own health in check, my own self-care up to date, so I am leading the ship with gusto. Think about what you eat? I am not going to pressure you to start eating only fruit and vegetables, to not have fun. I am asking you to think about choosing the majority of your food as healthy options. Make sure you eat five portions of fruit and vegetables. Drink water, eat protein, see your doctor and go over a healthy regime to make sure that you are feeling well and energised. Go to get your hair cut, go for walks, go swimming, do not put yourself at the bottom of the list. I lived on a very tight budget as a young student and mother. I managed to find bargains, vouchers, and ways of treating myself. If I can do it on that budget, you can too. There has to be a way and you need to find it as you are saving the world, remember?

I know you have read this in a lot of places, you open social media and someone is exercising and telling you how to lose weight or gain muscle. You look at meal plans and hear your friends telling you how much weight they have lost. We are bombarded by it. The simplest way to get healthy is to love yourself. Think about what is right for you and aim to feel good.

This is where I share the next exercise with you. I would like you to get out a notebook and do this exercise. Sit down and write out what you want for your physical self, your mental health, your work life, and your home life.

I'm going to tell you about one of the most powerful techniques that I learned from Joshua Sprague, a fantastic writing coach. He is an inspiration, and you can find him on Facebook and Instagram, his courses are amazing.

It's called the Pomodoro Technique and it was invented by Francesco Cirillo in the 1980s. Joshua made me aware of this technique and it is truly fantastic.

He carefully explained to me how it works. You set a timer for twenty-five minutes. During that twenty-five minutes, you put your phone on silent, you close the door, you tell anyone in your house (especially kids) that they are not to disturb you unless it's a life or death emergency and then you start the timer.

You just write. I mean, get into the flow. You can use colours, art, doodles, but keep getting stuff down, you have to get the words out and let them go onto the page so that you can really look at them.

'Why?' you might ask. Well, because forcing yourself to continue to write, even if it's terrible writing, will eventually drive you to a free-flowing state where you are now writing from your unconscious mind and you are really listening to what is inside. Do it and you won't be sorry that you did. Go do it now. I do it on a weekly basis. I teach the children at school to do it.

Do not think logically; think with your subconscious mind. Let it flow and you will be surprised at what arises. Your body knows exactly what it wants to get out there. Our conscious mind holds onto anxiety and worry. It can trap us into very anxious thoughts. When I am in fear mode for a long period of time, my body puts on half a stone. I have no idea how, but it seems to cling on to every calorie. When I am happy, my body naturally stays at my optimum weight.

If I am sleeping well, my body responds well to that. Your unconscious mind knows exactly what you need to let go of, release and feel better.

I did this exact same exercise that you have just done, and I discovered that I always wanted to write this book. It has been with me for so long. I knew I wanted to change something with my diet and my health, and for animals, so I really wanted to be a vegan. I was a vegetarian for most of my life, and I wanted to go vegan but was too scared I wouldn't know how to do it. It is actually so easy. I wanted to have success with my body and mind. I wanted to let go of certain pain and let my body and mind be healthy.

There are very simple things that you can do to help self- soothe. Yes, that's right, we can soothe ourselves. Who knows us better than we know ourselves? I love walking, but sometimes I think, *Nope, I am not leaving the house.* I have to tell myself, Get outside, you will love it, and without fail, every time I go out into the fresh air and walk, I feel better. These are things that you know yourself. Some people like to run, I am not a runner, but I love walking. I also love swimming; it is a big self-soothe for me. I love going to coffee shops. What do you like? If you feel it soothes you and is healthy, then do it.

There are obvious self-care routines that we all know and should follow: drink water, sleep well, sit in the outdoors, meet with positive people. We know all these things, but we also need to put them into our well-being lists. We need to do them, so our children are aware of how to do them.

I have to confess I got it majorly wrong as a young mum and made so many mistakes with self-care. My son was totally confused about what was healthy. I told you earlier I would go days without eating...how sad must that have been for him. When having the second child in my thirties, I had learned a lot about myself, about self-care. I was able to actually carry out these self-care lessons, so he could see and witness. I wish I had done this sooner and not waited so long. I am hoping I can help you to start this now as your life will change beyond recognition and your children's lives will be filled with happiness.

I used to get very ill when I was a young adult. I was probably unwell every month—cold, cough, sore throat, sickness. Self-care means keeping the body's immune system strong. Eight years ago, I started to take vitamins, and I now drink lots of water and look after my mental well-being. Don't think I live like a saint now; I do have coffee and I do have vegan chocolate and I do sometimes sit on the sofa for a day! I am human after all, but I would say most of the time, I am looking after my health.

Exercise is one of the most important self-care, self-love routines we can give ourselves. I don't mean forcing yourself to do something you hate, but something you love. I hate running, but I love swimming and dancing. Find an exercise that you love.

I wanted both my children to experience the freedom that swimming gives you. When I dive in and go underwater, my problems disappear. I am like a mermaid. I feel disconnected from the world and become free. My unconscious mind forgets everything and I skim the bottom of the water like an ethereal being. I encouraged both boys to swim from an early age and to experience this freedom. Exercise is one of the biggest self-care steps that we can take. I love swimming and I taught both boys to swim. The first time around, the oldest son would jump into the water and loved it straight away. I taught him to swim very quickly and the local pool was our happy place. So, after my second baby, I decided to get to the pool as quickly as possible. I hit a wall with this though, the second time around with my younger son, but I knew that I needed to persist as it was the ultimate self-care gift that I could give my children. When my younger son was little, every time he went into a pool, he screamed. Everyone, and I mean everyone, told me not to take him. I knew how much swimming would benefit him. I am not a believer in expensive swimming lessons; I wanted to teach both my boys to swim and have gone regularly with them once a week since they were babies. Both are very strong swimmers and love the water.

The little one, however, took a few years to convince! Every time we approached the water, he kept screaming and people kept staring, so I made a plan. We joined a small health club. It was reduced fees for three months and so it was very cheap. Most health clubs will do you a deal that works out to the same price as going to your local pool three times a week. I took him for ten minutes at first. Just holding him and telling him I would not let him go. So, for two weeks, we went for ten minutes three days a week. It was the summer holidays, so as a teacher I had six weeks to do this. Anyone reading this who is not a teacher, just remember you can still do it at the weekend. We built up to half an hour without him screaming and of course, as the weeks and months went on, he started to want to go to the pool. I had shown him my own joy, stayed calm, and he was then able to enjoy the water. I have no idea where his initial fear of water came from as both my eldest and I love swimming. It is still his happy place now if he is feeling a bit stressed with school. We go swimming and we are both laughing at the end of it! If you think this is not possible with more than one child, then think again. I helped a client to do this with twins! As I have said before, if you really want to do something, you can find a way!

Creating boundaries and sticking to them is an important part of self-care. I had a colleague who was constantly asking me to do her work. I would say yes; and she would ask me to take care of her two sons. I said yes, of course, I did. Her praise was like a hug for me. I felt worthy, good enough. One day she asked me to do something, and I had been invited to a party. I said no and she became hostile.

I blamed myself and I cried, kept saying sorry. I woke up one day and suddenly thought of my six-year-old self and I wanted to protect her. I rang the colleague and said I am sorry, I won't be doing those things anymore. I was a tired, single mum and trying to help her too. She was married and, to be honest, barely ever said thank you. If you don't set your boundaries, then you are not loving yourself. Set them with family, friends, and your partner. My eldest son's father was a charming lothario, older than me, and very good at getting people round to his way of thinking. I lost myself and he was happy for me to do that. I left him as I was not prepared for my son to lose himself too. If you don't have a self-care mind-set , then the people who are drawn to you are those with the same lack. They will then feast on your low self-esteem to take away the pain from their own shortcomings.

Both my children have fantastic friends, and they have boundaries. I am very proud of them as it means they are raising their own self-esteem. Think about it. Are your boundaries tight? Do you ever put yourself and your needs first? This doesn't have to be always but sometimes, really ask yourself if you want to say yes to a particular request. If you say yes, will it mean you are left tired and worn out? If you can't say no for your adult self, do it for the six-year-old who still resides in you. Do it for your own children who see you and learn from you. Do it today. At first, it is frightening and uncomfortable. Remember, you are the captain, and the shipmates are looking to you. If you need help learning to do this, get yourself a therapist or coach who will help you. Remember, your good mental health means a child's good mental health.

As well as scheduling time for your child, schedule time for yourself and your self-care. This might be a hot chocolate and a bubble bath. It might be watching your favourite soap. What do you like doing? Today I want you to find some time for you. I give you permission to have at least fifteen minutes off and this must be every day. If we all love ourselves, then the world is a happier, healthier place. The people who don't love themselves hurt others. The cruellest relationships I have been in (romantically and platonically) have been with people who have low self- esteem. These people have no self-love and have not witnessed it or know how to engage in it. If you show yourself love, then you are doing the whole world a favour.

I used to feel guilty if I spent money on therapy sessions; I used to berate myself. But I suddenly realised that after each session, I was healing, and guess who else was healing? My children were too, so actually, the £50 a month was really split three ways. Well, more ways, actually, as it made me a better daughter, friend, teacher, and the list goes on. I was helping a lot of people, not just myself. So think of something you want to do and put it on your list. Go on, remember you are saving the world!

If we don't have self-care, we overeat, we drink, we abuse ourselves, and we look to others to make us happy. Let me tell you this now, in over forty years on this planet, no one can make you happy but you. You can be around positive people, you can do lovely things, but the only person who can make you feel good is you. If you can show your child this, then you are setting them up for a lifetime of happiness.

I have met so many people who say they can't afford to indulge themselves. Remember about making excuses? I had very little money when I was a young mum; I was at university, had a small child and two jobs to keep us going. I contacted the local college who use students to cut hair, give facials, etc. The cost was around £3 or £5 at the most. With this in mind, I would treat myself once a month. My son would come in his pram and I would treat myself to some attention. I promise you that you need this. Whether you have multiple children, or just one, if you are a single mum or have a partner, you need some time for you. You need some time for a pamper appointment, a cup of tea in a café, a day out in a museum, but you do need it. Please give it to yourself and don't feel guilty. What makes you feel happy and healthy makes your child feel happy and healthy.

It is not indulgent; it is necessary. It is vital for your whole family's health. I am going to ask you to book something or some time to do this, today or this week. Do not put it off. You will feel lighter, younger, happier, and it will impact your whole family.

Now, this bit of self-care might be the hardest for some of you. It was hard for me. Letting go or not getting involved with toxic friends and family. How hard is it to recognise? In my case, very hard! We have to work with some people who are not our favourites, but we don't have to be friends with them or be around family who are toxic or not good for our health. Draw a line, ask yourself some questions. Who makes me feel good? How do I feel after I have been with this person? If it is not good, then you need to pull back. I will talk more about healthy relationships in Chapter 8. It is very important that you act as a role model in how to have effective, healthy relationships in your life.

I had a client, a lovely young man aged about twenty-one. He came to me as he said that he found family parties really difficult, but he felt he was expected to go. I asked him to tell me about it and he said he couldn't define why. So I asked him to try and find the place in himself that feels uncomfortable. He had an uncle that told him he was skinny and in his mind, that meant he was unattractive. He had an aunty who constantly compared him to his cousin; he had two cousins who spoke about themselves all the time. He had a sister who treated him as though he was something that was dirt on her shoe. This made me so sad and we had to make a plan which made his life happier. We decided that a fair compromise was to only attend two family parties a year, and after that, he would not attend anything else. He had to draw boundary lines. He also decided that he was going to have a good line for his family if they said something which he felt was not correct, or hurtful. It took some practice, but he started to feel happier and less guilty. You need to draw, lines that suit you. Get rid of people on social media who are not helping you to feel better. Keep your boundaries tight and keep yourself happy.

I had been drawn into the allure of an influencer on social media. I had not followed my rule of going by my gut instinct, instead, I merrily followed him, even though I felt some of his courses were dubious. The first course he sold was £100 and I bought into the hype and, to be honest, it was not good. There was barely any information and I didn't feel good about the content. I did message him and question what the course had actually been about. He fobbed me off and showed me all his great reviews, so of course, I felt I had been the stupid one. Red flag right there. I should have gone with my own feelings and trusted them. He sold me a few more courses and by then, my boundaries were out of the window. He was a fairly well-known work and emotional help coach, and extremely rich. I kept thinking if he is rich, he must be good. I was forty-one at the time—why on earth did I think being rich must equate to being good!. He was offering some great courses just after Christmas and they seemed to solve every problem you ever had. Every day he would post how great his life was and was really selling himself. I asked about one of his platinum courses and the cost was £7000. I asked if there was a cheaper course or a way of paying in instalments. He became quite mean and almost made me feel guilty for asking. He told me to put it on a credit card. I don't use credit cards, but he was actually encouraging me to go into debt.

You might think at this point I would have stopped following him, but my self-care was at a low, my boundaries were non- existent and I thought he must be better than me because he was rich! I carried on following him, but something didn't sit right for me. In his posts, he was all 'Love you all, love to make you happy,' but in real life, he seemed a bit like a money-making shark. Suddenly the penny dropped and I had an aha moment. I put myself first, realised that he was a waste of my energy and time. I had wasted £300 on him and he was a money-making shark. That is not me. I am very open, and I like to help people. Money is not my end goal, but it seemed to be his. I stopped following him and I felt lighter. Some people continued to buy into it and of course, that is up to them. But I personally did not feel he resonated with me. *I am not* saying you can't charge for your services but to make it so unavailable to the average person while writing 'Be free, anyone can take my courses, it is available to all' was not really true. It was available to those who had £7000 floating around in their bank account. Self-care, draw your boundaries and go with your gut instinct, things will soon fall into place, and you will happier and lighter! So then will your children.

Who resonates well with you? Who do you feel good around? Who lifts you up? I had a friend that would come and tell me every time I put on weight. Oh, you have put on weight, or You don't look good today. In the end, I just couldn't take it anymore, I felt like my whole life was revolved on how I looked and what she thought of me. If she told me I had lost weight, I would be euphoric. That is not a healthy friendship. I am lucky that both my children have healthy friendships. They have really good friends who are more like family. I will go further into healthy relationships in Chapter 8.

I was at university when I went on teaching practice. I had to shadow a rather ferocious teacher. She told me off in front of the children and it really upset me. She told me I was stupid and clumsy. I was very young, and I went into the toilet block and cried. I then went to see the headteacher, who told me I was too sensitive, and this teacher was trying to help me. I had the courage to go to my lecturer who went to see the school. He told them that I was an A-grade student and an A-grade teacher, he knew this as he had observed me twice, and he would be moving me to a more supportive school. I was moved and had the loveliest mentor called Emma. My lecturer told me my relationship with others was unique and amazing, he said to remember this: 'Your sensitivity is your strength.' I had the most marvellous lecturers at university; my favourites were George, Dudley, and Michael. They all gave me such confidence and help.

I always think of my old headteacher who used to say the world is changed by your example far more than your words. I believe that is true. If you are living by example, then the world will follow. Confidence is being yourself and being happy with that no matter what. The African saying of 'No enemy within, no enemy without' is so true. It means if you love yourself, then no matter what anyone says to you, they cannot hurt you. If you don't like yourself and already harbour an enemy within, then everyone's opinions can really, really hurt you.

My younger son does not let anything get to him. I remember once when he had not been invited to a party. It was a friend's thirteenth. He was very laissez fare about it. He was resilient and decided if he wasn't invited, then he wasn't supposed to be there. Look for the sunshine, not the clouds. You will see it if you try. We get hurt, we rise again, we try and we try and we keep learning. Be thankful for the gifts of learning and growing. Without pain, we cannot grow and be happy. Teach this to your children.

Self-care is important, self-love and awareness are vital. Look after yourself, stay hydrated. Sleep for at least six to eight hours per night, more if you can. We need sleep to function. If you are feeling that things are hard, then break them up into small chunks. If tasks look like mountains, break them up. I will often do this. I will put the washing in, do some hoovering, then have a ten- minute break to text some friends or have a coffee. Then do another bit of housework, some ironing, and then go and have some self-care, walking, meditating, then maybe some marking, etc. Do what makes you happy, but I find breaking up tasks or things that are not so pleasurable but necessary really helps me to get them done. Also, never be afraid to ask for help. Never be afraid to live in your own power and be you. Once you do, then so will everyone else. You are giving permission to everyone else to live in their power. I teach this to my children, the children in my school, those I see in therapy, and those in my family. I love you. You have got this, dear reader. Don't forget the worksheet for chapter 6!

CHAPTER 7
STOP COMPARING

I am what many people would call a yes-person; I have wanted to please people since I was very young. I want to say yes all the time in the hope that people would like me. Mainly because I felt I was not enough. I wanted affirmations that I was thinner, prettier, smarter, wealthier, funnier ... the list goes on. I constantly compared myself to others. If I lost weight, I would look at my thinnest friends and compare. It was exhausting. I was in a race I could not win. I was worn out from starving myself, comparing myself, and just living a life of looking at the person next to me. It was very harmful because guess what? Yes, you know the answer by now; your children start doing it. My eldest son finds it impossible to accept a compliment. He has done extremely well academically but says, 'Oh, the exams were easy,' or 'It was a fluke.' He compares and compares and who do you think he learned that from ... me.

I have always valued education and I mean all of it. Not just the academic side but the holistic side of it. I was at a girls' grammar school for a year. I hated it and my parents took me out of there. I felt completely stupid. I was with a class of highly academic girls where I was always in the middle. I was then moved to a comprehensive school—in the UK, this is a state school. I was happy there until I wasn't. I was constantly unwell with flu, asthma, and I was painfully thin. I missed a lot of school. One day I went to take a biology test. I had studied for it and wanted to please the teacher. Her name was Mrs Pearce. The question was to name all of the muscles and bones in the leg. I had learned the whole body, so I answered the question, but then I also drew the whole skeleton—just to please her and show her that I was working lots at home.

On the day the test results came out, she asked me to come to the front of the class. She told the class I had zero in the test and was the most stupid child she had ever taught. This was the 1980s, not the Victorian era! I have never forgotten that day and I believe that it really impacted me. First of all, I lost a lot of confidence, and I didn't care about biology. Who does that to a twelve-year-old? It later made me determined to become a different sort of teacher, a better teacher. Every class I teach, I look at those children and I ask myself, *How would I want my two sons to be taught?* and that informs every lesson I give. I wanted to be the opposite of Mrs Pearce and I wanted to let children know I cared.

In my third year of teaching, I was lucky enough to have a boy called David in my class. His mum was lovely and so was his dad. They both had a very competitive streak and were constantly pushing David to do more. He was a brilliant sports student, but he didn't enjoy academics. They were so adamant that he should do better academically. Of course, we should encourage our children to be everything they can; I am not debating that, but some of us are good at or better at different things and that isn't always academics. David was getting more and unhappy and it was impacting his grades and his demeanour. David's dad told me he went to Oxford and he wanted David to do the same. I know this would have been terrible for David. He told me privately that going to Oxford would cause him so much anxiety that he would be in total despair. I really wanted David's parents to talk to him, take his ideas on board. Listen to your child and encourage them but do not force them; it just isn't fair.

Think about how often you compare; you look at other people's lives and think, I want that. I should be doing that. I should look like that. I often used to compare myself to married couples—I am a single parent. How was that going to work out? Well, I was down on the numbers! So, one day, my younger son said to me, what have you achieved? How far have you come? It made me think, and I actually went and wrote it down. Now it's your turn. You can do the same in your lovely sheet at the back of this book. Write down what you have achieved. It could be simple things such as this:

I have a job.

I have friends.

I have a fantastic smile that lights up a room.

Think about what makes you special and what you have set out to achieve. Write it down on the worksheet marked Chapter 7. Go for it, and really enjoy this task. You can carry on doing it daily or weekly, whichever you prefer.

Now give yourself some goals. These are good as they make us wake up and think about what we want. Remember, they are your goals, no one else's. I can't have the same goal as the people next door, I am me, and they are them! When I first started teaching, there was a boy who had to have his leg amputated. I was horrified when I heard, and I cried for days. He came to school one year after his operation in his wheelchair, smiling and laughing. One day I spoke to him with tears in my eyes, and he said, 'Miss, I'm ok. We all have our own race, our own journey. I don't compare myself to people with two legs because that is pointless; I compare myself to me.' His goal was to be a lawyer and eventually walk with a prosthetic leg. He was not comparing himself to anyone and his only race was with himself. He is twenty-eight now, walks, is a lawyer and is also engaged. Set your goals and stick to them. This race called life, this journey is only with yourself.

My beautiful friend Nanda is five foot tall, takes a UK size 3 shoe and is a size UK 6 dress. I am five foot seven, size 7 shoe, and I will never be a size 6, so there is no point in me killing myself to do so. My goal is to stay healthy, be happy, and reach my own goal of being able to swim 100 lengths, get my message to the world through my book by the end of the year, keep my children happy, and keep the young people of the world feeling positive and good about themselves. My goal is to make *you* happier and feeling better. Choose your goals, write them up and keep aiming towards them.

Please don't compare your children to other people's children. It is very harmful and ask yourself if you would like it. Imagine if I said to you, 'Mrs Perkins up the road is much funnier, prettier and more successful than you.' You would just give up and go home. It is always good to say to your children what they have done well, and then you can help develop their goals. I do this in my teaching and the kids respond really well. I have a student in my class who has dyslexia. She and I laugh as sometimes she will spell something and it looks so funny that it makes us both giggle. If I want to support her, I start off by giving genuine compliments (always be authentic). I say something like, 'Well, I love the ideas and you have written lots.' This means she knows that she is doing well. I then ask, *How do you want to move forward?* or *What can we change?* I pick a small part of her work to focus on. She might say there are three spellings she thinks she has got wrong. So I give her a goal: *Let's aim to get those three words correct next time,* and she feels happy and positive. Don't overwhelm yourself or your child. Don't give yourself insurmountable goals; this is off-putting, and you won't do them.

Write yourself some goals today but also write down what you have achieved, what you like about yourself. Don't wait for others to compliment you. If you do this, then your child will be in the habit of doing it themselves. I once wore a dress to work that no one commented on. I have unusual taste, sort of bohemian meets Topshop meets hippy. I have been the same since I was thirteen years old. I loved watching fashion programmes and emulating the styles. No one commented on my lovely new dress I wore to work, but I loved myself in it; I felt unique and different. So most importantly, love yourself and don't worry about what anyone else thinks.

I worked with a man who constantly compared himself to others. He told me the story of how he went to see a house with his wife and they both loved it. I was excited and said, 'Why don't you put an offer on?' and he said, 'No way.' I was so confused. He said, 'Those people have had two people to see the house and we are the second, why would we make their life easier by putting an offer in? That didn't happen to us, so why make their life easier?' I was so shocked. This man was seriously going to give up his dream house as making an offer too soon would make the sellers happier...He was the kind of person who would compare his cake slices, his salary, his children's accomplishments...it was tedious and people stopped wanting to go for lunch with him.

Stop comparing. As humans, we do this all the time. It is dangerous, mentally harmful, brings our energy down, and it makes us feel like staying in bed. If you compare yourself to others, you will always fall short. Not because you are not as good as anyone else, but you will find fault in yourself. Remember, you are showing your child how to feel happy in their own skin.

You are unique. There is no one with the same DNA as you, no one who is you. Our fingerprints are all unique; no one has the same in the whole wide world. So why compare? Guess why we do it? We do it because we are feeling insecure. And it projects onto our children. We learned it from our parents; they learned it from theirs.

I met up with a friend from university one day. I was a single mum struggling to make ends meet. She had met a lawyer and he had a child who was lovely. My friend and the lawyer got engaged. I was happy for her, but I was also; Why not me? Why can't I have all those things? I am not proud of it, but I did feel envious. She married the lovely guy and became pregnant. We lost touch. Two years later, he was found guilty of hitting her and his child. One day he hit her so much she hit her head on the floor and died. It was tragic and affected the town so badly. I had no idea she was living in an abusive marriage and that her life was so awful. I felt guilty for losing touch. I felt a myriad of feelings that took me years to get over. Please don't envy others as you have no idea what they are facing or going through.

No one's life is perfect. I can promise you that. I know that as a therapist, a teacher, and as a parent. Children tell teachers everything and we know the parents who are shouting, storming out, drinking too much—they tell us. As a therapist, I see the people who look outwardly perfect and are crumbling inside. I once had a lovely lady come to see me as her husband was addicted to many things and she just couldn't cope anymore. Outwardly she was lovely, attractive, had a good job, well-dressed, and seemed the epitome of what we all wanted to be. She suffered with IBS, back problems, and asthma, which she believed all to be stress-related. You have no idea what others are going through. I can safely tell you that the people who criticise, shout and are generally mean are living a life of unhappiness.

No newborn baby is born miserable. No new-born baby looks at the other babies and thinks, *His cot is better than mine.* We learn these things; it is learned behaviour. No child is born to compare. Babies learn from the adults, and they learn quickly. Hypnotherapy can bring you right back to your very early days and really help you clear the clutter.

I saw a quote on a poster once in a café in Brighton. It said 'Remember being happy doesn't mean you have it all. It simply means you're thankful for all you have'. I have tried to live by that quote. If I am feeling low or things have not gone to plan, I have a few hours of feeling a bit sorry for myself and then I say, 'Ok, what is it that you do have?' I have a great family, have two jobs I love, I have my health. That is a good starting point. Neville, my darling friend who died at a young age, used to say to me, 'You have got everything. Your smile, your good heart, and your laugh...' It summed it all up. We were just friends, never in a relationship, but his love for me was one of the greatest I have ever felt and it will go with me forever. I wish I could have done more for him, but I know as a teacher I can now lookout for the Nevilles of this world, those who are mistreated and need the love of us all.

I am giving you permission to be happy in your own skin. I want you to change your language. If you have given birth and you have stretch marks, cheer for them. You have carried babies and those are your reward. If you have not carried babies but have children and you see a few lines around your eyes, cheer because those lines show you care. If you have some grey hairs, another cheer, you are Wisdom itself.

No one has lived your life and your eyes tell a million stories. You are your own story. No need to compare as you are delightful and beautifully unique and just you.

Tell your children this. Give them this gift of not comparing. Let them enjoy every minute of being themselves. Let them enjoy themselves and be happy. Let your inner child enjoy being happy. Do you know the most desired guy in Hollywood in 2017? It was Jack Black. He is not someone who visits a gym or has his hair done every day. He is funny and happy in his own skin. He is cheerful and delightful to watch and I hear on the grapevine a great guy to be around. If we are happy in our own skin, then life changes. We change, our children change and so do those around us.

So I am going to ask you to do this from now on. If you should happen to start comparing, you can sing in your head 'Stop,' or you can sing out loud, up to you. Or you can sing 'Stop! I love you,' but just stop. Say these words to yourself: 'No more comparing for you (insert your name),' and then name three things you like about yourself. I am currently writing this book in my slippers and old cardigan, with my rabbit on my lap. I could look at my social media and compare myself to others, but oh no...I am going to quickly list three things I am grateful for about being me. I have great slippers; my rabbit is very cute, and, of course, I love writing this book and it is unique to me. Train your mind, jump in, and stop the comparisons. I promise that life will change and so will you.

When your child starts comparing themselves and saying 'It's not fair,' do the same. No matter what their age, sing or say the words to one of those songs and tell them to tell you three things they like about themselves. They might say nothing, so you will need to help them out!! They will try to tell you those positive things aren't true, but deep down, they are listening, I promise, and you are making a difference.

I used to look at the sensible teachers and think I should be more like them. I was always comparing myself to my colleagues. I have always been the slightly zany, funny teacher. I had a child in my class who used to come in feeling really miserable. Every day I would sing good morning to him and make him laugh. Every day he would tell me to stop. One morning I was not feeling too well so didn't sing it, he didn't say anything. I assumed he was relieved as he always looked embarrassed. He was fourteen at the time. I was packing up to go home that evening and he had just come from a football match. 'Miss, why didn't you sing this morning?' I looked astonished, 'I have a sore throat. I thought you found it embarrassing?' He looked at me and said, 'I do and I think you are absolutely mad, but I don't want you to stop.' I said to him, 'Mark, I thought you might like a sensible teacher like Mrs Holmes and that you found me embarrassing.' He laughed and replied, 'No way, Miss.' How funny—so he had enjoyed it and missed it. I had compared myself to another colleague, thinking that my students would prefer her, but in the end, they liked my unique style! Kids like you to think you are embarrassing them or that they are not bothered, but they like it when you are happy and when you are their cheerleader. Lesson to myself: just be me and be the teacher I would like to be taught by!

Children need us to be happy and to show them the way. We are the captains, and the ship needs to be sailed with a whistle and a few songs. All of us are doing our best and that is all we can do. The trouble is that if our children are not happy, neither are we. It is a catch-22: we need them to be happy, so we can be happy...but truly, we need to show them how to do it first.

Comparing ourselves is time wasted. Train your mind and the minute you start comparing, do the trick of breaking into song out loud or in your mind. Laugh at yourself. If you start comparing, start to laugh. Make fun of yourself and it becomes a joke. If you see the neighbours drive into their drive in a BMW, smile and say how great for them and be happy for them. I drive a small car but, do you know what? I love my little Aygo car. It is fun, easy to park, and great. Why am I even comparing it to a big bulky BMW? Laugh, dance, sing and just let it go. It is good for your kids, for your health and for that little inner child you care so much about.

Pets have a great way of making us realise that comparison is not needed. Do you have animals? If not, go and look outside or go for a walk. I have three cats and an indoor rabbit. I look at them lolling about and they care for nothing but their food and being cuddled. A friend came to my house and he said, 'Oh dear, your rabbit is not the prettiest.' I was not very pleased, but I looked at her with some of her fur missing and her slightly weird eyes and I thought, *You are wrong, she is the most beautiful rabbit in the whole world.* In my mind, I listed all the things she does: she goes up onto her hind legs for a bit of popcorn, she chases the cats, she licks my hand, she rules the house, and is totally perfect for our family. She does not care if her fur is missing—all she knows is that she is totally spoilt, fed on time, and spoken to like she is the Queen of Sheba. Strangely enough, while writing this book, one of my cats, the elder male, stands by the keypad. He snuggles up to my hand, expecting to be stroked and adored. He knows that he is loved and obviously feels he is the favourite. They are all my favourites, but he presumes he is! Cats are so confident!

Animals don't compare and they don't think, *Look at Dibbles; he hasn't been to the gym in a while.* Stop comparing and criticising and you will feel lighter, better, and happier. It is just so easy, cheaper than a holiday, and you will feel so good. Go for a walk today and look at the trees, each one beautiful in its own way; no two are the same. Nature can teach us a lot.

I am going to ask you to have a go at all of these. While you are out in nature, have a go at some earthing. My children and students think I am completely mad, but I often take off my shoes and socks and walk around on the earth. I also hug trees! If you do it and laugh at the same time, your children will see it is ok. It is ok to be a little bit silly, to have fun and be at one with the outside world. You are perfectly imperfect, and you are you. I hope that I get to meet you all one day and see how amazing you all are. You are creating the future generations and their happiness; you are changing the world and I love you for it. Now go off and hug some trees and smile as much as you can. Get your children smiling and this gets the world smiling too. It is infectious and contagious in the most brilliant and wonderful way. You have got this and I am proud of you.

CHAPTER 8
MODEL HEALTHY RELATIONSHIPS

I used to run a very lovely drama academy. I had been running it for over twenty years, since I was very young. I started it in my first year of university to help children gain confidence. It also provided an income for my son and me through my university years. One day I decided that the children needed a meditation day. We all sat down and just closed our eyes and meditated for five minutes. Then I gave out some paper and we had to write the first words, thoughts and dreams that came into our heads. I wrote: I want to be a therapist. I was completely shocked. Where on earth did that come from? I had no idea. I sat with the idea and the next day, an email came through asking if I would be interested in studying extra courses. I had filled in some mental health awareness forms a few months ago. They say that the teacher arrives when the student is ready, well that is exactly what happened to me.

I rang up about the courses and they were a mixture of online and in person and would take two to three years to complete them. There was no funding, so I had to take out a small bank loan. I was so excited, and I eventually trained as a therapist, hypnotherapist, life coach, and mentor. It was hard work and I carried on working full time throughout. I am not sure how I managed this and look back and ask myself, 'Tara how on earth did you do this.' I have to laugh sometimes as I have no idea, but I do just carry on and keep on going. I came out with distinctions and then I set about seeing clients on a Saturday. I do the two jobs that I love, teaching and helping people. I have had to have my own therapy as some sessions have triggered me. I am getting better at not letting things stay in my mind but there are some clients that will stay with me forever. The greatest joy I have had is using hypnotherapy with my father. When he was diagnosed with dementia and his legs started to fail, I used hypnotherapy. He has had amazing results. I am forever grateful that I was able to train and help him. My parents were very supportive of my training and urged me to do it. They knew it was something I loved and, just like teaching, it has been a calling for me. My dad always asks, every day, 'How is the hypnotherapy? You are going to change the world.' His words always move me, every time he says them. Our relationships with our parents and grandparents inform the way our children treat us. They watch and they want to do the same as us. So, think about that very carefully.

I got a call from a man called Richard; he needed therapy as he was struggling with his son David's departure to university. Richard and David had been very close until one day they had a huge falling out over curfew times. David started to distance himself from his father and when he went to university, would only text or call his mother, Suzy. She would say to David, 'Your dad is right here, want a word?' and her son would decline. Richard was so distraught as they had three daughters and only one son. He told me that he and David were more like best friends. Richard and Suzy had David at a young age, when they first met at university, and then waited five years before having more children.

I started to ask Richard questions about his relationship with his own father, Lucas. He looked down and said his father was stubborn and not easy to get along with. He admitted he hated phoning his father and only saw him once a year, if necessary. Richard's father was now in his late seventies and it seemed too late to change things. I asked Richard if he could or would consider inviting his father down for Christmas. Richard shook his head, 'No way.' I asked him to consider it. Time went on and I thought Richard had decided against my idea, but he told me his dad was travelling down from Birmingham on the 23rd of December. I was delighted and asked him what he liked about his dad. He responded, 'Nothing.' I said to him that there must be something. He replied that they had liked doing jigsaws together. I asked him to consider doing some jigsaws again with this father.

Christmas came and went, and Richard came to see me in January. He was slightly less weary and said that, in fact, he had had a good time with his dad. He had completed two jigsaws and learned how his dad had fainted at his birth! It was unusual for those times for a man to be at the birth of their child, but his father had insisted. I said that was very progressive of him. Richard laughed and said 'Yes, he is more interesting than I thought.' Lucas was still stubborn, but Richard decided to ignore some of his comments and focus on his relationship with him. He started to call his father more and even suggested him coming at Easter when David would be home.

A year later, David and his father Richard were back to speaking and even started going fishing together. I asked Richard what changed, and he said I had changed things for him by showing him that anything is possible and relationships can be fixed. Richard had changed his relationship with his own father and David was emulating that in turn. Children watch how we treat our parents and, at some level, will do the same. They may not even do it consciously, but they will do it ultimately. Think about the way you are with your parents and then you may see aspects of that in your children.

This goes for all relationships and friendships. If you want your children to choose wisely, then you must too. I often used to choose friends who were quite unkind to me. I had a group of friends from an NCT group (the National Childbirth Trust is a UK group for parents) whom I met after having my eldest son. All the women were about ten or fifteen years older than me and affluent. I was a student and poor! I remember we went for a meal with the children and the waiter brought back the change. One of the mums tossed it to me and said, 'You have it, you are poor, you need it.' Maybe she hadn't meant it in a mean way, but, unbelievably now, it seemed acceptable for her to speak to me like that. I felt that was what I deserved. I clung to these NCT mothers like a lifeboat. They wouldn't invite me to things at the weekends with their husbands because I was a young single mum. They would drop their children to parties and look at where I lived like it was a hell hole. I called these people my friends. My son went on to choose similar friends at primary school.

I was called into his Year 1 class one day and his teachers told me that he was being bullied. I asked who was doing it. They said he wants to be friends with some older children, but they keep hitting and pushing him. At an unconscious level, he was emulating me. Find friends who are not right for you and persistently try to be friendly with them and your children will do the same.

So how do healthy relationships begin? How do we recognise them? I always like to see the best in people, but I have learned now that we must trust our gut instinct. Our intuition. Why does this matter? I believe we inherently have the ability to tell if something feels 'off' or is not good. I tried to tell my younger son about this, but he seemed to say it wasn't a 'thing', but I have ignored my instincts so many times and then found out, to my detriment, that I was right in the first place. I remember having a head of department who everyone loved. It seemed she was the nicest person in the world. I kept having dreams that she was wearing a mask and something about her made me feel uneasy. Two years later, it turned out she was changing the marks on exams, just for her class, to make herself look better and was sacked. Everyone said, 'We can't believe it, not Sara,' but I could believe it because everything about her made me feel slightly 'off'. Go with your instincts and I believe you can't go wrong.

All your relationships are under a microscope with your

children. They learn from you, the good, the bad, and the ugly. When my dad was diagnosed with dementia a few years ago, I had to think about how I'd reacted. Everyone that knows me will tell you that I am a crier. I cry at sad films, at animal cruelty, etc. You get the picture. I feel sensitivity is my strength as I have a lot of empathy for everyone. This is very good in my jobs as a teacher and therapist.

When both my parents told me about my father's prognosis somewhere deep inside of me, I knew that crying was not the right option this time. I knew that whatever I showed at this time was vital, this would either help or hinder my children and my parents. So I took a deep breath and said, 'Ok, well, at least we know.' Some of the family went and read everything about it and then were utterly miserable, but I decided on a different approach. I was going to celebrate what time I have left with my dad. Me being miserable would not help my parents or my children. Write it down, share it with other friends, pray, meditate, whatever gets you through, but find a way of dealing with it in the most positive way possible, as this will be the thing that gets your children through many ups and downs that life offers.

My father is a role model to my sons. He is someone who provided for his family and gave sage advice. He and my mum have been married for over fifty years and are very much in love. They are a team and work well together. They are very traditional in many ways, and it works for them. They are best friends and embraced dementia with positivity. Dad has become a little frailer, especially after Covid, as it seemed to make his dementia worse, but he is still here. I can still cuddle him and laugh with him. Dad used to hate animals but now has fallen in love with their new kitten, Fluffy. My dad seems more smiley and quicker to laugh.

If I started to feel miserable from the day he was diagnosed I would have missed out on all of this 'fun dad', but more importantly, my children would have heavy hearts. Your reaction, your happiness, the way you deal with relationships and life will be engrained in your children's minds. As I mentioned, as a very young mum, I was constantly 'not dealing with things and people' and all this did was make my son so miserable.

Help people out, help in charities, do kind things. If you are doing the right thing, then your child will too. You honestly can't expect your child to do the right thing if you are not also. You *want* them to be moral, upstanding citizens. Well, guess who they learn from? The captain of the ship and that is you, the adult.

I had a lovely lady visit me in therapy who said that she argued constantly with her sister. The lady was called Shona and her sister was Linda. They argued over everything. One day the whole family went away together. They had three brothers, and partners, children, and their parents all went. It was supposed to be the holiday of a lifetime to celebrate their parents' fiftieth wedding anniversary. It was a disaster, and mainly because the sisters fell out and then so did their partners and then finally the children too.

Shona had come to see me as her children would not stop arguing, so much so that the youngest boy had ended up at A&E.(emergency unit of the hospital) It was really worrying, but I had to ask her to look at the dynamics in her own extended family. Shona and I spoke for ages about this and she signed up for coaching. I asked her to look at how much she argued and squabbled with her own siblings, and she was perplexed. I said that the cousins and siblings are emulating what they see in the adults around them. She had an aha moment and promised to repair the relationship with her sisters or at the least make it less argumentative. I can happily report that they all went away together last summer and it was harmonious. Apart from grandad falling in the river, but that was not an act of aggression, only him having too much fun!

We get back what we put out. When I was about seven years old, I was extremely lonely at school. I didn't speak to anyone and was very shy. I found it hard to reach out to people, but I knew I wanted friends, but never felt good enough. I was the only mixed-race child at school, I felt self-conscious. The only time I was popular was when the children sang 'Brown girl in the ring' and they put me in it.

If I saw someone fall over, I would be off getting the school nurse. I was that sort of child. I liked helping animals, people, insects, etc. I spoke in a tiny voice but always wanted to be kind and do the right thing.

One spring day, just before my eighth birthday, I saw a butterfly caught up in some string at school, and off I went to save it. I turned around to see a little girl called Lisa behind me. She had an American accent. She was the most popular girl in school. She had a twin, and they were living in the UK for six months for their father's job. They had cool accents and cool lunchboxes, and everyone wanted to be their friend. They especially wanted Lisa (the taller of the twins) to be their playmate as she was so enigmatic, and people just loved her hair and her clothes and her smile.

Lisa was just about to turn eight, like me, and said that she had watched me saving that butterfly. She said she liked saving things too. I just nodded and smiled and went to get my pencil case. She followed me and said, 'Would you like to be my friend?' I blinked and blinked again. She said, 'You are the kindest girl in the whole school.' I was completely unable to speak, but I felt a rush of pride. On that day, and those that followed, we became inseparable. She told me that she wished I was her sister as she felt like I was family to her. We were so happy together and I felt like this was the first time that I had been loved by someone other than my family.

Other children stared in envy that Lisa was my best friend. I went to her house, and she came to mine, and we spent every moment together. I had given out kindness and it found me tenfold. She returned to America and I never saw her again, but she left me with the knowledge that I had experienced a very healthy and beautiful friendship. It was the first time I recall being really loved by a peer.

Since that day, I have used Lisa as a benchmark. Does this friendship make me happy? Am I comfortable in it? Does it align with my own values and feelings? Sometimes we have to ask ourselves is this friendship right for us. We do that and we teach our children to do the same. If you tell your child, 'Oh, little Freddy is not nice,' and then we hang around with people who are not nice then that is just useless. Actions speak louder than words and this should be true for you. Also, strive for the Lisa-type friendships. Strive for the ones that make you happy. Your inner child, your actual child, your mental health are calling for you to have healthy relationships. Have a healthy relationship with yourself and this will lead to having loving people around you.

This brings to mind an incident that happened to me where I was in a conversation with a very pleasant, albeit a little self-centred, lady and we spoke for an hour. I learned a lot about her, but I doubt she knew anything about me. I asked questions and was genuinely interested. I love finding out about how people tick, what is on their mind and their goals. She asked me one question: 'Where do you work?' That was it. She later told my other friend how lovely I was and easy to speak to. I had barely said a word! When you meet a friend or you are out at a party, are your conversations one-sided? Are you the listener and perhaps taken for granted? I have taught my children to show a genuine interest in people, really care and ask questions that show that, but also to choose friends who care and listen to them too! This makes them a good friend, but they also choose wisely and are the kind of people that others want to be around. Make sure they are around good people too, not like the lady who spent her time talking at me. Make sure they are in equal relationships, not all give and no take, but totally equal.

If you are on social media and you have 2000 friends whom you never speak to, lose some of them. If you have people on your phone whom you text, but they never text you first, then give yourself a break. A friendship should be a two-way thing; it must be reciprocated. Ask yourself if your friendships are like this?

When I moved house with my younger son, he asked me to make friends with the neighbours. I am still very shy and my answer was a big fat no. He looked disappointed. I suddenly realised that I needed to do this to show him: 1) I would push myself out of my comfort zone. 2) We have good people around us. 3) We are part of a community (very important for children in a single adult household, makes them feel safer).

So, I went and bought some little cards and put them through our neighbours' doors. Hi, how are you, etc. What happened next was that we made a lot of new friends, and we had a community. In fact, when we got Covid, those same neighbours left food parcels and checked that we were ok. I had reached out and my son saw this. I felt much better, and I also felt very glad that we had moved.

I would like you to think about connecting with a neighbour or friend at work and inviting them for a coffee or a walk. Making new friends is invigorating and fun. It can be nerve-wracking, but there are many people out there who you don't know yet.

There are a lot of good people in the world, despite what the media try to show us.

We need to show our children how to make good friendships and be a good friend. We can only do that if we do it ourselves. It isn't always easy and can take a lot of willpower to push yourself out there. What have you got to lose? I find by writing a note or email then the person can think about it and if they don't want to, then that is fine. I always think that handwritten notes are so personal and make people feel loved.

Make yourself feel loved; the people who are your friends feel loved, and your child will feel it too. Most of us just want to be loved and be happy. You have the power to spread that into the world and then your child will too. Show them how to have healthy friendships. Show them how to behave with friendship groups, parents, grandparents, aunties, uncles, cousins, family friends. Show them rather than tell them and they will learn a lot more quickly. My longest friendship is thirty-five years and I am proud of that, but I have made many lovely friends in my life, some friendships have been short-lived and some have been ongoing for twenty or thirty years. Whatever their length, I am happy to have them in my life.

To finish this chapter, I am going to ask you to think about how happy it makes you to be friendly and to sometimes be a little vulnerable. You feel proud, you smile more, and you uplift your own energy. You uplift your own life. If you complain about someone, are miserable or not friendly, it is bad for your blood pressure, causes extra lines, and just makes those around you miserable. More importantly, it makes your child miserable.

Their happiness is paramount to you and, therefore, it has to start with you. Every morning I put on calming music for my students as they come in. I care so much about their happiness that I have brought rugs in, plants, and have the walls covered in happy posters. I want them to feel nurtured and I hope my setting up this environment, along with me smiling as they come in, will give them a good day. Remember, everything you do and say in friendships, with work colleagues, with your family is being watched by your child or the children in your life. You are the captain and your actions speak volumes. You can do this, go out, smile and laugh. Do this for your inner child and every child in your life. You have got this and good luck with being happy! You own this and it is in your power to change your world and those around you. We impact so many people every day and our moods and optimism ripple out to hundreds of people, so think about that as you smile your way to changing the world. We are here and now is the time to live our life to the full.

CHAPTER 9
LET GO

My friend sent me a card which said: 'Happiness begins with you. Not with your relationships, your friends, or your job. But with you.'

Sometimes we grasp happiness or grasp onto others, hoping that it will bring us joy. It always comes with a caveat of that person or friend or boss being in a good mood. Have you ever just tried to let go? I mean, really just let go. Lie on the floor and just relax your whole body and laugh...try it. Just let go and see what happens. Some things we just can't change or help. People will do as they please and they will follow their path and sometimes this hurts or makes us angry, but if we let go, we free ourselves up to feel love and be loved. Put on a meditation or relaxation video on YouTube and let it relax you, just let go. Disconnect from all of your problems and give your mind a break, a holiday from it all.

My client Daisy came to see me in November. Her parents were divorced, and she was getting married. Her two sisters were really not supportive, and Daisy was trying to get her parents to agree on the wedding and how it would work with the bridal table. Her mum still blamed her dad for leaving; her father was mild- mannered and just wanted peace and quiet. The sisters didn't care and just told Daisy to sort it out. She had started suffering severe back pains. I felt so sad when I saw her walk in. She is a lovely person, pretty and outgoing, but her back twinges were making her limp and stoop. I told her that she looked as though she was in pain. She said she was! This was her second marriage; and she had two teenage daughters who were also suffering with headaches.

Daisy had two hypnotherapy sessions and six life coaching sessions with me. She was carrying the responsibility for everyone, her daughters, her wedding, her parents. She just couldn't walk with the burden of it all. Daisy was a nurse and was used to caring for people. I asked her what her daughters wanted to be, teacher and nurse, she said. I felt like her little family were all carers, people who wanted to give and not expect anything in return.

Daisy and I did a lot of work on her past during our coaching sessions. As mentioned, I also gave her two hypnotherapy sessions. I asked her what would happen if she let go? She started to shift in her seat. 'Let go?' she asked. It was like I had asked her to hold up a bank. She looked really nervous, 'Let go,' she said again, looking shocked. I asked her to tell me what would happen. 'Everything would fall apart, and everyone would be unhappy because of me,' she said. I told her that the only people she was responsible for were her daughters and her. She could love and support her extended family, but her first priorities were her children and her own health. I told her to take the girls out for the day. She replied that she had no time. I said if she didn't then she wouldn't be walking down the aisle. Then she said she didn't have the money. I said just go for a walk and get an ice cream and spend time together. Then I said to her, 'When you get home, lie on the floor and let go, give yourself the freedom to just care about you and laugh and smile.' I told her to then watch a funny film and enjoy herself.

She wasn't convinced this would work. She had my audio mediation recordings and she was also doing gentle yoga with the most fantastic yoga teacher in England, Francesca Corcoran (www.yogawithfrancesca.co.uk). Daisy came in the next week looking five years younger and with very little back pain. She smiled and I said, 'What happened?' She said, 'I let go.' I asked, 'Did anyone die?' She replied, 'No, no one.' We then talked about what the family had done when she let go. She said that at first, they kept asking why she wasn't sorting out the wedding and then they said she was being selfish. She said that her therapist had told her to have time with her daughters and let go! Her back pain went. Her sisters had to sort out the row with her parents and she let go of the reins and just enjoyed being in her own power.

Who is holding you back? Who is keeping you stuck? Let go today, right now. I don't mean just let go of all responsibilities but of worry or emotionally manipulative people who are holding you captive. Let go and give yourself some space. You are entitled to a life and, if you don't believe it, I am telling you that you are!

So right now, go and lie down and take three deep breaths. Smile and smile again. Laugh if you want to and say to the world, *I am letting go*. Feel the ease in your body and just let life happen; you don't need to hold on to worry, you can just be you and you are entitled to happiness. I promise you that.

My children used to get very anxious about things, especially at night, and I used to say, 'Just rest now, let go and just think about lovely things.' This seemed to calm them down. A few years ago, I was worrying about my friend who was in hospital. My younger son came into my room. It was about 8 pm, and he said, 'Just rest, let go and think of lovely things, Mummy.' I laughed as he was repeating what I said to them in similar situations. My worry was not going to help my friend or anyone else. It was not going to help my health. I let go, I was calm, and I thought of lovely things.

If our children see us letting go, then they can too. Who has negative influences on you? Do certain friends on Facebook make you feel in a low mood? Unfriend them. What about those who come and tell you all their problems and there is no reciprocation? Choose to find other friends. Choose a group that lifts you, keeps you happy. Your children will do the same. My children have really lovely friends, and I really enjoy it when they come to the house. If your children mix with good friends, then they will have good times. You will worry less when they start to go out independently as you know they will be with good people. Remember your children copy you; if you are letting go, choosing uplifting people, then they will do the same.

Also, don't be too vehemently against their friends if you don't like them. My dear friend Mel rang me to tell me that her son, Ronan, had come home with a girl with a tattoo that said 'I hate authority'. Let me tell you, though, that there were a lot of swear words also involved in this tattoo. She smoked in Mel's house and swore in front of Ronan's brother, aged eight. Mel told Ronan he could never see her again. Red alert, wrong thing to say to a seventeen-year-old. If you are against their friends or partners, then you are building a wall. I told Mel to invite the girlfriend round and be very supportive. If she swore, just ask her nicely if she could not do it in front of the younger sibling. She did all of this and after a few weeks, Ronan decided he didn't like the girl as she swore at an old lady, and he felt uncomfortable about that. Also, he said that he had nothing to rebel against (his mum liked and accepted his girlfriend) and it felt pointless being with her. I am not saying be supportive of them doing anything dangerous or detrimental to their health, but if they bring home a partner you don't like because you don't think they are quite good enough for your little darling, then go with the flow, if this person is not a danger to anyone. Saying no and storming out will make your child more likely to stick with this person just to prove a point!

Let go, smile and let the world flow with you. Also, be happy for others. Spread the joy and see the magic happen. A few months ago, a lovely lady came to our school. Her name is Georgina Jones. She has written a fantastic book called *Turn Lights On*. She is also a coach and speaker. Look her up; she is amazing and lovely in real life too. She says if we are in a shop, or perhaps in a queue, ask the person next to you, 'How are you?' Make them feel special and magical. I do it all the time to shopkeepers, strangers at Costa, and it is amazing. But if you are not convinced, try it, guess what it does for you? It makes you smile, and you go with the flow. Human connection is imperative, makes us feel alive. Children watch us interact, turn lights on, and they copy us. They feel happy. We feel happy; the world feels happy. Try it. At first, I was so nervous and cursing at Georgina Jones, thinking this won't work. I was in Aldi and I asked the man scanning my food, 'How are you?' He looked at me, 'Very well, thank you.' He then made a comment on my vegan food choice and we had a nice little conversation. He said I was the first customer who asked him how he was. Show you care, feel the love and let's pass that love around the world.

I had lost touch with a dear family friend. He worked with my father and his children were friends with my children, my parents love him, and we had spent some lovely times together. We lost touch and I thought it was the end of our family friendship. Sometimes when you start spreading love and happiness, it finds its way to you. My journey of spreading love and happiness led to us all getting back in touch, and he has been like a brother to me, uncle to my children, and ever-giving to my parents. Let go and let the world change you; let go and smile, spread love and see what happens. I cannot tell you how to live your life or what to believe in. I pray and give thanks, but you may have other methods. Whatever they are, let go and trust that you are being looked after and the world is a good place filled with love. Connect with people; make a difference and the love you will receive will be priceless. Your children will cherish these loving connections and they will understand how the world works. They will understand that connection and love are the most important things.

I am not saying skip about like Pollyanna; I know there are people who will still be unkind, and I have had my fair share of unkindness. I do say that you need to let go of that hurt and pain; let it go now. Don't let those people live in your head. Wish them well and carry on with your loving-kindness. I was in a clothes shop when a stunning woman was trying on a dress. Some of the other women were looking at her with slightly sneering looks on their faces. I just wanted to tell her how lovely she looked. That is exactly what I did. Her face froze, surprised that I would say it and then she broke into the biggest smile. 'Thanks,' she said, and seemed really pleased. My son said, 'I thought that was going to be embarrassing, but she was really happy.' Celebrate each other; we are here on this earth together, build good healthy connections and live your best life.

So as Georgina taught me when I first met her, start turning lights on. She challenged me to turn five lights on that very day. I rose to the challenge and did it. My son was impressed with me. I give you that same challenge. Turn five lights on. If you are at home, go and connect and give someone a true compliment or ask how they are. If you are going out, do it five times to shop assistants, café owners, and people ahead of you in the queue! It gives you a natural high

I went to a quiz with both my sons. I had been turning lights on all day and I was practically giddy with excitement. The quiz master thought we were siblings and kept referring to us as the youngsters. I had literally lost fifteen years off of my face and was glowing. I walked differently and was more confident and connection with others meant I felt better in myself. If you want to learn more about turning lights on, then go buy Georgina's book.

Another fantastic person, who I mentioned earlier in the book, is Tracey Stone. She gave me the most powerful and enlightening feelings through a hypnotherapy session. She is a fantastic author and therapist. I have learned so much from her and she also glows from the inside out. Tracy has the skin of a thirty-year-old and the smile of an angel.

Connection and finding our comfort group is imperative. Who we hang around with inspires our children. It lifts us, and we feel better, we look better, and life becomes less scary. If you are less vehemently hard with your children, they will be more likely to communicate with you. They will be open and tell you things. I believe that my relationship with my sons and those I teach has always been open, and they talk to me...I hope that will continue. Also, be prepared to say sorry. If you get things wrong, then admit you have. If children are able to say to you that you have hurt them or you made them feel upset, listen and apologise if you think you got it wrong. Don't be defensive or dismissive. If your child can communicate with you then you are going to have a happier, healthier child.

I came in once and put the dinner on. I was really feeling stressed as I had so much marking to do, and I was so tired. My younger son made a comment about the house being messy. I was so upset, and I felt so defensive; it brought up triggers and made me cry. He was astounded, and quite frankly, so was I. I don't shout at my children or my students and very rarely lose my temper, but I was really inexcusably angry. I went upstairs, washed my face, and came back down and apologised. I explained how I was feeling, and it cleared the air. I feel apologising and opening the door to communication is imperative. I know a lot of parents won't apologise, but if I have acted in a way I am not proud of, then I am the first person to say sorry. I want to acknowledge it, own it, and apologise for it. This makes your children feel safe; they feel loved and listened to. Don't make them feel you can't be spoken to, or if they get it wrong that you will not admit your own fault in the situation. Teach them how to be good people and then you will raise humans who will bring only happiness into the world.

The last bit of the chapter is about something that has been really hard for me. I really have struggled with not being invited to things or my children not being invited to parties, etc. It opened a wound early on so deep that I thought I would always be like that. One important thing I have learned is that if people don't invite you to something, say a silent thank you, they are not your comfort group, and you are not theirs. Saves you wasting an evening or an afternoon. It also frees you up to spend time with your wonderful self or with others in your group. You like you, don't you? That is all that is needed. Teach your children the same. Not everyone will want to be your friend and not everyone will want to invite you to things or events, be ok with that. I know, I know it is not easy and I really struggled with this one but remember... let go. If you don't get invited, let go of those angry, hurt feelings. You cannot change it and accept that they are not your group. That is ok. It is not a reflection of how great you are or how great your children are. Teach your children resilience. When we have self- love then we learn not to take things personally.

I remember at our old house when a new family moved into the neighbourhood. They invited everyone to a party on the street, except for us. I was really upset for days. Then I found out the party really wasn't my cup of tea, and I was so thankful that I hadn't been invited. They were not my group. We recently moved to a new home; the neighbours are very like-minded. We have good chats, and we socialise. They are people that I want in my group, and I am more comfortable with them. If someone doesn't invite you to something, then they are not people who you would bond with, so it is better to wish them a lovely time and go and do something wonderful that you like doing.

Remember, you are unique and so is your child. You will always be special and wonderful. Put this as your screen saver, or on Post-it notes, but remember it. Not being invited to something does not make you less wonderful. Write that somewhere, so you remember it. Let go, let life go on and be happy. Let your physical body relax, enjoy life, and give your children the example to do that too. You can't be responsible for everything and nor should you be. Sometimes you just need to let go and let the world do its thing as you rest, relax, and smile. Worry is a waste of time and effort and changes nothing. Laughing, on the other hand, makes us healthier and happier and changes us inside and outside. I would say that is a much better result. So now go off and do something wonderful, for you and your children! I am proud of you; keep going; you got this. You are more powerful and stronger than you can ever imagine and sometimes doing nothing but having fun is the most powerful thing you can do. I give you permission to let go and have some fun times!

CHAPTER 10

CELEBRATE EACH DAY

We have reached our final chapter and what a journey it has been. Remember you can use this book and the exercises at the back as often as you want. Use the book and re-read it when you feel the urge to feel happy. I mean, it is a conscious decision to be positive and feel the joy. I know that there are dreadful things that happen, I am not for one second saying that you can sing and dance yourself through trage- dies, but I am referring to general life, which has its ups and downs and these come with choices. See them as terrible or reframe them. It is your decision; you are in control of your own thoughts.

Imagine your mind is a small puppy and it needs to be trained. Choose to train it and to reframe and look at things in a positive way. Guess who else will do this? You guessed it, your child. I worked with Flossy, a lovely bouncy little girl whose mum was so worried about everything. Molly, her mother, came in saying that Flossy had 'terrible' sleep patterns. She said, 'Flossy had a disastrous time at school.' These words were not helping Flossy, who started to become as worried as her mum. I asked Flossy what was happening and she went on to tell me that she didn't like the dining hall as it was too noisy, and she also didn't like the school lunch- es. I was really interested to see that Flossy was also using words such as disgusting, awful, and terrible. The first thing I said to her was, 'How brilliant that you are able to define and tell me what is going on. Lots of ten-year-olds aren't able to say what is making them feel unhappy. How amazing are you?' She seemed really pleased about that. I then started to change my language. I said, 'Gosh, your school sounds full of very excited children, but I understand that might be a little overwhelming at times.' She nodded and her body language changed. 'So, how could we make you more comfortable?'

'I like some areas of the dining hall as it is less noisy but still has some interesting conversations, so maybe I could sit there.'

'Great!' I said. 'That is a good start.'

Her mum said, 'But it is all too much for her.'

I said, 'Let's see if we can ask if Flossy could try out sitting in the corner she likes. Would this be possible, to ask her teacher?' Molly seemed a little worried, but after persuasion, she said she would. Then I said, 'Could you bring a packed lunch, Flossy? And perhaps you could help your mum make it. I bet you are good at cooking?' Flossy was beaming at this point; it made her feel really grown up and she said she would love to do that. Molly began protesting, 'But I don't think she is old enough.'

I said, 'You can help her and give her some ideas on things which are nutritional.' I also asked Molly if she would like a hypnotherapy session. She said she wouldn't, but I said that it was there for her if she needed it. She eventually took me up on my offer and after two sessions, it seemed that Molly was really struggling. She had hated school, the noise, and the lunches. She had been badly bullied, and her mum had been a career woman who gave Molly no support. She felt that if she didn't support Flossy, then she was a bad mum. She was holding onto Flossy as she had felt so unloved as a child and scared herself. She was so frightened of dropping the ball and missing something that she wanted to control every aspect of Flossy's life.

She felt when Flossy was unhappy that it was a reflection of her; she felt she needed to micromanage everything. She sat and worried all day and the biggest thing she did was project her own fears onto Flossy. It then became 'their' problem. It was a shared disaster and Molly became more and more anxious. How many times do all of us project, onto our children, onto our friends, and even every day when we interact with people?

I was told once during my therapy training that as people, if we actually understood how frequently people project onto others, we would all learn to take absolutely nothing personally. We project all the time. Think you don't? How many times do you say to your child, 'Put a cardigan on, you must be cold.' Must they? Or are you cold? How many times do you imagine that you know what someone is thinking, 'You must think I look a right wreck.' You go to an interview and say afterwards, ' I know they hated me.' To whom and when are you projecting? Think about it because every time you do, your child feels it and will respond in the way that is really just cementing your fears.

My younger son started at a new school knowing, absolutely no one. I was petrified and started thinking about my own fears. I didn't verbalise them but, as we know by now, children pick it up. But I decided I was going to reframe this: 'This is going to be a great new start, a chance to get some lovely new friends, join new clubs.' I raved on about the advantages of starting a school knowing no one, the chance to see who you might like to hang around with, someone who has the same ideas and interests as you. Anyway, of course, it went well. I changed my language and I stopped projecting my own fears onto him. I stopped outwardly, at least; I am a mum, after all; I still worried a little bit inwardly on his first day at secondary school! I worried less when I changed my language. Change your words and see what it does. Try it today.

Start changing the way you speak to yourself if you are saying things like, 'I hate my job, I hate my friends.' It won't help. Children learn from you and listen. It also does make you happier. If you can't reframe, how can they? Who will they learn from? It has to be with you, the captain of the ship, the leader. The first hero in their lives.

So, how do we celebrate each day? As mentioned, I am not talking about days that are truly awful, someone dying, or tragedies which are truly heartbreaking. I am talking about everyday life, even times like divorce. I went through a bad divorce, but I tried very hard to find a positive in each day, even if it was just that I got dressed that day. I am asking you to celebrate everything that you can. It can be tiny, or it can be large but celebrate it each day and really start to feel good!

My children have seen me dance around the room, sing, and clap if something goes well. I believe life should be celebrated big time, readers. I know there have been times I have been miserable and this, in turn, has made my children miserable, so I am very aware of finding the good in life. When my father was diagnosed with dementia two years ago, you would not believe the number of people telling me how 'awful' it was. I was astounded. I decided to celebrate the time my dad was able to remember me. I see my dad most days and most days, we laugh. He is still very much himself and for me, it is a case of taking each day as it comes and living in the moment. Some days he is forgetful, but he also remembers a great deal, and that is what I focus on. I write down all that he remembers rather than highlight all that he forgets. My mum is very loving towards my dad, and she too celebrates every day they have together, and that is the way it should be.

Celebrate what you can, find the good. It is believed that stress-related illnesses are the third biggest killer in the western world. Suicide in males under fifty is one of the top five killers in the west. How frightening is that? We are all responsible for our society, so now is the time to start the change, start reframing, finding the good.

Even during lockdown, I tried to find the good, celebrate each day, and was thankful I was still alive. If you don't, what is there? A life of gloom, frown lines, and illness. Happier people live longer, get fewer diseases, and are a great example to everyone. Stand in your power, make the rest of the world sit up. Who is that happy person over there? Ah yes, it is you!

At my last school, I made the decision that I was going to make as many people happy as I could. This would be teachers, students, all staff. I started a Fun club. This was a poster I put I put on my classroom door: 'Fun club runs Friday and Monday lunchtimes. If you want to come along and feel happy, then sign up or just pop your head in. There will be lots of l laughing and lots of feeling better.' How did this progress? Wonderfully, I can tell you. I didn't include things like 'we are going to meditate and talk about our problems' on the poster. I just put that we are going to have fun. So, the club took a different approach every time we met. We sometimes just put on music and danced for an hour, sometimes we went outside and took off our shoes and let the earth heal us, and sometimes we played funny games and told jokes. Sometimes we just celebrated a good thing that had happened. We celebrated, we smiled, and we felt better. I felt better, the children felt better, and it was a wonderful, powerful feeling. Some of the teachers that came along left looking like they have had a holiday.

If someone criticises you, change it around. Ask yourself, what is that person projecting onto me? Think of all the positive things that people say about you. Think about someone who loves you and what they think of you. Turn it around. I came into school with three broken toes last year. The children were upset, and everyone was saying, 'Oh no, that is terrible.' I said, 'No, it isn't as I have this groovy boot to wear and I have all of you lot running around doing things for me.' Smile, laugh, and change the story.

A parent called me about my Fun club. She asked what I had done to Amir, why was he so cheerful now in the mornings? What happens in this club? What is the magic? I invited her to come along as I felt she needed to get a bit of that happiness. It is catching; it is amazing, just try it.

In another of my previous schools, there was a young lad who had some difficult times. He was very angry one day and

I was very close to taking him to see the headteacher as he was so cheeky in class. He suddenly broke down and told me how his dad had left, and his mum was depressed. I felt so upset and just wanted to adopt him on the spot! I very slowly taught him how to reframe things, and bit by bit, he began to feel differently. He thought that the reason his dad had left as he, the child, was so horrible! He started to understand that he had nothing to do with his dad leaving. We started the 'cheer you up club' which eventually reached forty-four teenagers!!

I also have had happiness mentors in my classes. These are people I have trained up to take happiness around the school. They were criticized at first for being a bit 'see the good in it all' but it worked, and half the school were seeing the best in their day. Take the bad as a lesson and learn from it. Then take the good as the things to celebrate. If I had not had the trauma I had as a child, I would not be a therapist or a teacher who connects so much with the children. I believe that my trauma was sent as a teacher for me to learn so I could then give support to others.

I got many things wrong, especially as a young mum, things I would like to change. I can't go back. I can only show my children and those I teach how to live and enjoy their lives now. You will make mistakes, we all do. This is when you need to forgive yourself. You need to move on. I have hurt my children and I have been immature, but I hope I have learned, albeit the hard way, to be a happier person, and in turn, made my children happier. I have learned to be a better mother, teacher, therapist, daughter, and friend. I find the good in everything I can, and I try to help others do that too.

You must forgive yourself for mistakes you have made. This is imperative. I have lay awake at night feeling guilty (especially about the hurt I have caused my eldest son), but it serves no one. I wish I could tell my teenage self what it was all about, but alas I can't. I can, however, help you and hope you don't make the mistakes that I made. I hope that I have many more years on this planet, and I can give others the benefit of my mistakes. I can pass on all that I have learned now and how it impacts those that I work with.

If you are nervous about finding a therapist or seeking help, don't be. It is the most wonderful thing. Try to go on word of mouth as I find that you need to know that person is good. I found my therapist through a friend. I was saying I need this, this, and this, and I was met with, 'I know someone who would be perfect for you.' My therapist changed my life, and I then went on to have hypnotherapy, also life-changing for me, and decided to train as a therapist myself. I also went on to train as a mentor and coach. Speak to the therapist, see if you feel comfortable. Don't be afraid to say that it isn't the right fit for you. I would not like to work with anyone who does not feel I am the right fit for them. As therapists, we want the best for you, remember that.

We are all born perfect and beautiful, and along the way, mud and rubbish gets thrown at us. We need to find that perfect us, under all that rubbish others have projected onto us. If it takes therapy to remove that rubbish that others have projected onto you, then do it. Don't feel guilty for spending the money on yourself. If you are spending £50 on therapy, divide that between all the family members you have. If you can't afford to pay for a therapist, then your doctor's surgery will be able to give you the number of a medical therapist, which will be free, or contact Wellness Stars for an appointment. Do things you love, do things which help your mental health. Get yourself into the fresh air, hug a tree, take your shoes and socks off and dance on the earth. Everything you do is helping your inner child, helping your adult self, and, of course, helping your children.

Your child may be five or twenty-five; this works whatever age they are. It is never too late to make these changes, to make yourself happy and to make them happy. I know it can work as I live it every day. Surround yourself with positive people, not mood hoovers who bring you down. Find your positive group and mix with them, dance with them, and be happy.

Now we have come to the end of this book, I would like you to promise me, and more importantly, promise yourself, to stay with the ideas in this book. There will be days when you feel like you want to stay in bed. Be kind to yourself on those days. Treat yourself as your own best friend. Get the book out and read it again. Say to yourself that I am commanding you to feel loved and feel happy. Tell yourself you have that right to feel happy and cherished. Stop imagining fake scenarios and hurting yourself. If you imagine that the world hates you, that you are wrong, or that you are useless or that people think you are, stop those thoughts. Live in the moment, live in the now. The last piece of love and advice I would like to give you is that you are the main character in your life. You make the storylines; choose your supporting actors and you are in control of your own thoughts. No matter what happens, how bad it gets, you can still choose your thoughts. When I was teaching, we had a lady visit from an educational centre; she had been in Auschwitz. She lost all of her family, but her mother had told her before she died, they can hurt us and be cruel, but we choose our thoughts; they cannot control the thoughts in our head.

I know life will throw things at you, that is the nature of being human. Please understand that you can always return to your default of love. Being resilient and choosing your thoughts will keep your children doing the same. Remember your power and remember your strength. I have not met you and I hope I will one day, but I know that my love goes with you on this journey. We are all human, all one, so my love for you is all part of this circle of society. Please choose to give love to yourself, your children, and those you meet. I would love to hear how things are going, how you have found the exercises. You can contact me on my website for ideas, therapy and feedback.

Remember you are the captain of your ship, lead it wisely,

lead it with strength, and do not be afraid to ask for help. Thank you for coming on this journey with me. I wish you all the happiness for all the children that are in your life, and all future generations. Be happy and spread that joyous ripple wide and far. You have the power, and you are a superhero. I love you, and I wish you every happiness that you can find. I look forward to meeting you one day.

If you would like to come along to one of Wellness Stars' workshops or have a one to one with me either in person or on Zoom, please go to my website:

https://www.wellness-stars.co.uk

You will be able to find out about me and the amazing Francesca Corcoron and her online yoga.

5 THINGS I LIKE ABOUT MYSELF

1. _____

_____

_____

2. _____

_____

_____

3. _____

_____

_____

4. _____

_____

_____

5. _____

_____

_____

Letter TO MYSELF
AS A TEENAGER

Dear _____

(fill in the name of your parent or legal
guardian when you were a teenager)

_____

_____

_____

_____

_____

_____

_____

_____

_____

_____

_____

_____

_____

_____

ACTIVITIES TO DO
WITH MY CHILDREN

Where we are going? What we are doing?

Agreed
Time Limit
& Budget

Monday:

Tuesday:

Wednesday:

Thursday:

Friday:

Saturday:

Sunday:

WHAT DO I WANT
FOR MY FUTURE SELF?

Mentally –

_____

Physically –

_____

Relationships –

_____

Home life –

_____

Work life –

_____

HOW FAR
HAVE I COME?

List 10 things you have achieved already

1. _____
2. _____
3. _____
4. _____
5. _____
6. _____
7. _____
8. _____
9. _____
10. _____

5 things you will achieve this year

1. _____
2. _____
3. _____
4. _____
5. _____

5 things you will achieve next year

1. _____
2. _____
3. _____
4. _____
5. _____

CPSIA information can be obtained
at www.ICGtesting.com
Printed in the USA
BVHW021722241022
650159BV00012B/214

9 781915 492586